MW00365128

The purpose of this study guide is to provide supplemental educational material. It is not intended as a substitute or replacement of SIX OF CROWS.

Published by SuperSummary, www.supersummary.com

ISBN – 9781679271793

For more information or to learn about our complete library of study guides, please visit http://www.supersummary.com

Please submit any comments, corrections, or questions to: http://www.supersummary.com/support/

TABLE OF CONTENTS

Published in 2015, Leigh Bardugo's young adult fantasy novel *Six of Crows,* the first in a two-part series, received starred reviews in *Publishers Weekly, VOYA,* and *Kirkus Reviews.* A fantasy heist story, the novel shifts between the alternating points of view of five teenagers who team up to pull off the ultimate prison break.

Six of Crows begins in Ketterdam, an invented version of 17th-century Amsterdam, and the novel's main characters hail from the seedy criminal district known as the Barrel. A people known as the Grisha, who originated in Ravka (the text's version of Russia), possess magical powers.

Plot Summary

Seventeen-year-old Kaz Brenner or "Dirtyhands," leader of the Dregs gang, is abducted by a merchant with a business proposition. The merchant tells Kaz of a new drug called *jurda parem* that, when ingested by Grisha, amplifies their existing power. *Jurda parem* is extremely addictive, and Van Eck fears governments could potentially control Grisha with the promise of more *parem* while using the Grisha's augmented powers to wage disastrous wars. The man who invented *jurda parem*, a scientist from Shu Han named Bo Yul-Bayer, is being held in the Ice Court, an impenetrable fortress in Fjerda.

Van Eck wants Kaz to break Yul-Bayer out of prison, so the scientist won't share the formula for *parem* with foreign governments. Kaz accepts Van Eck's mission, believing the reward money will help him take down Pekka Rollins, a rival gang leader who conned Kaz's older brother Jordie. Kaz gathers his crew: Inej, his right-hand woman, known as "the Wraith" since she can practically become invisible;

2

Nina, a Grisha; Matthias, a Fjerdan former *drüskelle* (Grisha hunter) with intimate knowledge of the Ice Court; Jesper, the Dregs' sharpshooter; and Wylan, Van Eck's runaway son who is also a skilled bomb builder.

The crew arrives outside the Ice Court and waylays a prison wagon, changing places with six of the prisoners so they'll be carted into the Ice Court's prison. Inej survives a harrowing journey up an incinerator shaft, and in the process, she finds a new goal for herself: she'll hunt slavers and their buyers. Jesper uses his Fabrikator powers—he is secretly a Grisha but has kept that fact hidden—to pull iron from the prison bars, and Kaz uses that iron to pick the locks. Nina and Kaz search the prison in case Yul-Bayur is in one of the cells, and Kaz finds Pekka in a cell but chooses to let him live.

An extra checkpoint of guards prevents the group from walking into the embassy as they'd planned. Inej and Nina disguise themselves as members of the Menagerie brothel to enter, while the boys use a secret *drüskelle* bridge Matthias shows them. Inej fights back against her former madam Heleen but is uncovered as a criminal and captured by guards. Nina tries to seduce *drüskelle* leader Jarl Brum into revealing Yul-Bayur's location. Brum captures and imprisons Nina, and Matthias pretends to be on Brum's side at first, but he eventually turns on Brum and frees Nina. Matthias and Nina soon discover Yul-Bayur is dead, and his teenage son, Kuwei, is being forced to try to recreate *jurda parem.*

Nina considers killing Kuwei, but Matthias argues that the boy has been robbed of his home and family just like the rest of them and deserves better treatment. They take Kuwei and meet up with Kaz, who uses an explosive made by Wylan to uproot the Ice Court's gigantic ash tree, revealing a spring through which they escape. The victorious crew rides all the way to the harbor only to find 200 soldiers and a group of *drüskelle* waiting for them. Kuwei gives Nina a dose of *jurda parem*, and she gains the power to command the soldiers, forcing them to drop their weapons and sleep.

When they return to Ketterdam, Van Eck meets the Dregs on a deserted island, and reveals he has no intention of giving them their reward; in fact, he plans to kill them with the help of *jurda parem*-dosed Grisha. The merchant kidnaps Inej and tells Kaz he has a week to deliver Kuwei, or Inej will die. Kaz asks the crew to join him in a new quest to get Inej back, and they all agree. Kaz's reassembled crew visits Pekka Rollins and asks for a loan to take revenge on Van Eck and reclaim Inej. As Kaz and his ultimate enemy, Pekka, make a deal, it becomes clear that more danger and deceit await in the sequel, *Crooked Kingdom*.

Chapters 1-10

Chapter 1 Summary

In the wealthy merchants' district of Ketterdam, a major port city in Kerch, a young guard named Joost patrols the mansion of Councilman Hoede. Joost had wished for a more thrilling assignment, but after an ambassador's recent assassination, the Merchant Council has increased security for "merchers" like Hoede. Joost passes the evening dreaming about Anya, an indentured servant to Hoede and a Grisha who possesses magical abilities. Anya is a Healer, a Corporalki Grisha who specializes in the human body, with the ability to stop the heart or snap the bones. She made a bruise on Joost's cheek vanish simply by touching it, and after the experience Joost fell hopelessly in love with her.

Joost enters the Grisha workshop but finds only Retvenko, a Squaller Grisha who controls winds to keep ships safe. Retvenko hopes Joost has information about Yuri, Hoede's Fabrikator Grisha, who fell sick and then disappeared after Hoede took him away for a mysterious mission. Joost doesn't know where Yuri is. Retvenko tells him Hoede has taken Anya away as well.

All guards are summoned to the boathouse, where Joost discovers a giant freestanding cell made of metal, with one wall of one-way glass. Anya, a small boy, and a guard are inside the cell, while Hoede, another mercher, and many other guards crowd around it.

The other mercher expresses concern about "what happened to your Fabrikator," and Joost realizes he's referring to Yuri, but Hoede assures him he's "lowered the dose" (10). Inside the cell, the guard cuts the boy's arm and Anya heals it by touching it; Joost and the others can hear Anya's comforting words through vents in the cell. The guard cuts the boy's arm again and orders Anya to swallow a powder inside a paper packet. She hesitates but does so; immediately her pupils dilate, and she smiles to reveal a tongue "stained like rust" (12). She heals the boy by waving her hand above him without touching him, something a Corporalki Grisha shouldn't be able to do. She demands that the guard shoot the glass. His expression goes slack and, under Anya's control, he complies.

Hoede orders the guards to capture Anya, but she commands the room to "wait." Joost is filled with an empty peace, "his mind silent, his breath steady" (14). Anya picks up the boy and orders Hoede to enter the cell, and he does so. Anya, her eyes "black and bottomless pools," commands Hoede to "pick up the knife" (14).

Chapter 2 Summary

Seventeen-year-old Inej Ghafa— "the Wraith"— approaches the Exchange, the center of trade. It's the heart of Ketterdam during the day and neutral territory in the city's gang war. It's night, and the Exchange stands empty, save for the crew Inej is meeting: 17-year-old Kaz Brekker, nicknamed Dirtyhands, the leader of the Dregs, and eight other members of her own gang.

Kaz mentions three ships sent to Ketterdam by the Shu, "stuffed to the sails with gold" (16), that will pay off the Shu's debt to the Kerch. He wonders if the Shu assassinated a Zemeni ambassador a few weeks ago. Inej herself had searched the washroom where the ambassador was mysteriously found with a knife in his back; the room had only one entrance, and no one else was inside. Kaz and Inej remain concerned with this puzzle but have more pressing problems on their minds.

Kaz and his seconds, Jesper Fahey and Big Bolliger, remove their weapons in preparation for the parley with a rival gang, the Black Tips. Jesper wonders if Kaz should give up his walking stick as well, but Kaz responds, "Who'd deny a poor cripple his cane?" (18). While Kaz and his seconds meet with the Black Tips' leader Geels and Geels's crew, Inej scales the Exchange to spy from the roof, with an agility and invisibility suited to her nickname. She watches as Bolliger pats the Tips down for weapons, and Kaz tells Geels to keep his gang away from Fifth Harbor. When Kaz became leader of the Dregs, he mortgaged the gang's previous venture, the Crow Club, to rebuild the harbor and revive it into a landing spot for merchant ships, tourists, and soldiers. The Dregs have dibs guiding the visitors—and their wallets—to the bars and gambling houses that the Dregs own in the Barrel, Ketterdam's pleasure district.

Geels reveals he's bribed two guards to kill Kaz and his seconds, and Inej begins inching around the roof, looking for these guards. Geels orders one of the guards to fire, and a shot from the roof hits Bolliger in the stomach. Geels continues to bluster but seems panicked, and Inej is sure the shot hasn't landed as planned. Kaz names the two guards Geels bribed and reveals that he uncovered the plot and lured one guard to his side. Geels orders the guard still on his side to shoot, but Inej reaches the guard and puts a knife to his throat first.

Geels pulls a pistol from his jacket and prepares to shoot Kaz. The Dregs realize Bolliger, who searched Geels but left the pistol, must have betrayed them for the Black Tips

(Kaz had suspected Bolliger was a traitor, and chose him as a second that evening to confirm it). Kaz says two Dregs wait at the home of Geels's sweetheart, prepared to burn her home if Kaz doesn't "walk out of here whole" (32). Inej is struck by the change in Kaz's manner as he makes the threat: "the monster [is] here [...] Dirtyhands [...] to see the rough work done" (32). Geels surrenders and agrees to keep the Black Tips out of the harbor. Even so, Kaz uses his cane to break Geels' wrists.

Kaz tells Bolliger he must leave town by sunset tomorrow, and Inej watches everyone leave from her perch on the roof. She sends the guard home and pities Bolliger, wondering if she should help him, but she concludes that "the Wraith [doesn't] have time for traitors" (34).

Chapter 3 Summary

Kaz leaves the Dregs celebrating while he goes to check on business at Fifth Harbor. He senses Inej "shadowing him" like the silent Wraith she is, and eventually she reveals herself and asks about the fire set for Geels's sweetheart. Kaz says there was never a fire—he was bluffing, which pleases Inez. Kaz notes that she often "wrings little bits of decency from him" (38).

Inej leaves, and a man attacks Kaz. When Kaz fights back, his ghost-like assailant seems to disappear and re-emerge, even stepping through a wall. Kaz wonders if his brother, Jordie, has "come for his vengeance at last" (41) as the attacker impales him with a syringe.

Kaz comes to in a luxurious room, chained to a chair, and recognizes from his captor's red laurel crest that he's Jan Van Eck, a Kerch merchant. Although Kaz has never met

Van Eck before, he knows Van Eck's house well, and he knows he's not in the mercher's house at the moment.

While Van Eck verbally reviews Kaz's arrests, the first of which happened at age 10, and Kaz's considerable list of crimes, Kaz works his way out of his chains, grabs a letter opener, and holds it to Van Eck's throat. The mercher's guards approach, weapons drawn. Van Eck calls for someone named Mikka, and a boy "pale as a corpse" (45) walks through the wall—just like the man who attacked Kaz. Mikka's coat identifies him as a Grisha Tidemaker, but even the magical Grisha can't "just stroll through a wall" (45).

Kaz demands an explanation, and Van Eck says Mikka has been drugged with *jurda parem*. A Shu scientist, Bo Yul-Bayer, created the drug and sent a sample to the Kerch Merchant Council. Kaz releases Van Eck in exchange for his pistol and cane, and the mercher explains that while any Tidemaker Grisha can control water and draw moisture from the air, *jurda parem* enables a Tidemaker to change himself or any object "from solid to liquid to gas" (47)— including a wall. Van Eck says the merchers gave *jurda parem* to two other Grisha; one, a Fabrikator, then transformed lead to gold.

Van Eck reminds Kaz of the Shu ship full of gold, probably created with the help of *jurda parem*, as well as the ambassador's assassination and documents stolen from a military base, all probably the work of drugged Grisha. Yul-Bayur, worried about the Shu misusing his creation, asked the Kerch merchers for asylum, but the scientist was captured and imprisoned at the impenetrable Ice Court in Fjerda. Van Eck wants Kaz to free Yul-Bayur—a possible suicide mission—and he will pay Kaz a fortune to do so. Kaz feels tempted; the money will allow him to pay his debt to Jordie and realize his dream. Kaz wonders why Van Eck chose him, and the mercher reveals he knows Kaz stole a valuable painting from him, and the theft convinced him of Kaz's criminal talent.

Kaz still wonders about the other Grisha to receive *jurda parem*, and as Van Eck begins to describe her, Kaz realizes they are in Councilman Hoede's house. Van Eck escorts him to the boathouse to see her work. The Grisha, a Healer and a servant of Councilman Hoede, ordered Hoede's guards to "wait" days prior—and they are still doing so, showing no reaction even when Kaz nearly shoots one in the head. The Grisha also told Hoede to cut off his own thumb and he did so, "smiling all the while" (56).

Van Eck describes this Grisha's fate: She stole a boat and likely headed to Ravka, but her body washed ashore. The Grisha probably fought against the current, attempting to return to Ketterdam for one more dose of *jurda parem*. The drug appears incredibly addictive, leaving the Grisha hooked after the first dose.

Kaz raises his fee for the job to 30 million *kruge* and Van Eck agrees. Van Eck reminds Kaz that if he fails to save the scientist and the formula for *jurda parem* is unleashed, "Kerch will not survive" (57). Finally, Van Eck wonders why Kaz always wears gloves. Kaz contemplates the many rumors—people say his hands are bloodstained or covered in scars, or that Kaz possesses demonic claws—and then demurs and tells Van Eck all the stories are "true enough."

Chapter 4 Summary

From her room on the third floor of the Slat, a house in the Barrel that Kaz has fixed up with his own earnings, Inej senses Kaz entering the building. Intent on eavesdropping, she follows him to the office of Per Haskell, the Dregs' official leader. Per Haskell berates Kaz for not asking permission before ousting Big Bolliger, whom Haskell considers his own soldier. Kaz tells Haskell he has a job that will make them "rich as Saints in crowns of gold" (64), and Haskell will get 20 percent.

Inej accompanies Kaz to his office, where he offers her a job for four million *kruge*, and she responds that "money like that is more curse than gift" (65). Kaz takes off his gloves, something he only does in front of Inej, who sees nothing wrong with his hands. He tells Inej to gather a few others so he can explain the mission to all of them, and he emphasizes she can take or leave this job—an unusual development. Since Per Haskell bought Inej's contract from the Menagerie brothels, Inej has been indebted to the Dregs and has to do what they say. This optional job appears different—and most likely very dangerous.

Chapter 5 Summary

Kaz walks through the Barrel, passing his own popular Crow Club and another gambling club that makes him seethe with rage: "the Emerald Palace, Pekka Rollins' pride and joy" (70). Kaz's desire to take revenge on Pekka keeps "Jordie's ghost at bay" (70); Kaz, already stealing Pekka's business and hoping to bring Pekka to "his knees, begging for help" (71), believes Van Eck's payment will help him exact his revenge.

Kaz enters the pleasure district and arrives at a brothel called the House of the White Rose, where he uses a peephole to spy on employee Nina Zenik. Nina, wearing the red *kefta* of a Heartrender Grisha, and her fully clothed client sit in silence until the man thanks her and leaves with "tears in his eyes" (75). Nina, a member of the Dregs, uses her Grisha talents to calm her clients' anxieties. Believing that her power over the human body will prove invaluable for his mission, Kaz tells her about *jurda parem* and asks her to join his crew. Nina, loyal to the Grisha and their homeland of Ravka, thinks Yul-Bayer should be killed rather than saved. She refuses Kaz's offer, but when Kaz says he'll help a prisoner named Matthias Helvar, Nina becomes more interested.

Chapter 6 Summary

Kaz, Nina, and a Dregs enforcer named Muzzen ride a rowboat to Hellsgate prison after midnight, all of them wearing elaborate costumes. Nina feels perplexed to see other boats with riders dressed for a party; she can't imagine what these masked people are doing at a prison, and Kaz won't explain his plan. They disembark at the prison and pay off waiting members of the Dime Lions gang. Inej, who snuck in on a supply ship, meets them inside.

A Dime Lion member guides them to an amphitheater, where the costumed audience watches prisoners battling fearsome creatures like a giant lizard with "wet, white, and foaming" (87) poison dripping from its teeth. Kaz explains that Pekka Rollins, leader of the Dime Lions, first conceived of this Hellshow. Nina recalls how, after she arrived in Ketterdam a year ago and testified in the case against Matthias, Pekka had tried to convince Nina to use her Grisha talents for the Lions. Inej also recruited Nina— who needed employment to stay in Ketterdam, since she refused to abandon Matthias—so Nina joined the Dregs instead. Since then, Nina has tried to convince Kaz to break Matthias out of Hellsgate, and she realizes now he's finally doing so.

When the guards bring Matthias out to fight, Nina sees that the boy who once seemed like "a shining savior with [...] eyes the pale blue of northern glaciers" (90-91) now seems hardened: "a killer." In fact, Matthias has always been a killer: He is a *drüskelle*, a witchhunter from Fjerda who once hunted down Grisha and executed them.

Matthias must battle three wolves, a terrible task since wolves are sacred to the *drüskelle*, but he kills all three. Nina sees that Hellsgate has stripped Matthias's eyes of anything human, and she blames herself. The guards take Matthias away, and the Dregs soon head toward him. Nina uses her Grisha talents to put a guard to sleep, and Kaz takes off his costume to reveal a guard uniform underneath.

Kaz picks the lock to Matthias's cell, and they find Matthias passed out from a sleeping draft. Kaz tasks Nina with recreating Matthias's wounds on Muzzen and making him appear to have firepox as well. Muzzen—who will be paid handsomely for this duplicity—will be placed in quarantine while the real Matthias leaves Hellsgate. That task finished, Nina heals Matthias, kissing his forehead with "the ache of tears threatening" (99). Matthias wakes and gently touches her face—then throws her to the ground and wraps his hands around her throat.

Chapter 7 Summary

Matthias dreams, as he often does, of hunting Nina. In the good dreams, he throttles her until "the life drain[s] from her eyes"; in the bad dreams he kisses her, hating the fact that "some sick part of him" still wants her (104). He wakes, sees Nina there, and begins to strangle her, but Kaz shoots something into his shoulder that makes his arm numb.

An uproar begins outside: According to Kaz's plan, Jesper has released the Hellshow beasts, and the group escapes to the boat where Jesper is waiting. Matthias attempts to kill Nina again, but Nina uses her Grisha powers to put him to sleep.

Matthias awakens in the Crow Club, surrounded by the crew from the prison breakout. Kaz explains their mission and asks Matthias, a Fjerdan with intimate knowledge of the Ice Court, to help, but Matthias refuses to "betray his country again" (111). Kaz offers Matthias the chance to become a *drüskelle* once more: Nina will recant her testimony against Matthias, and he will be pardoned for charges of slave trafficking while Nina spends two months in prison for perjury. Matthias thinks the punishment isn't enough for Nina, but longs to return to his home "without the burden of dishonor" (115). Even though sharing inside knowledge of the Ice Court will be treasonous, Matthias compromises his morals and joins the "demon" Kaz's crew, planning to hunt Nina and make her suffer as soon as he's free.

Kaz formally introduces the rest of his crew, including Wylan Van Eck, demolitions expert and son of Councilman Jan Van Eck—and as such, the group's "guarantee on 30 million *kruge*" (118).

Chapter 8 Summary

The crew argues over whether Wylan should be allowed to stay; because he's been to the Ice Court and has a talent for drawing, they decide he can. Wylan sketches the Ice Court as Matthias describes it—built on unscalable cliffs, with only one guarded entrance, two checkpoints, and an inner fortress of "concentric circles, like the rings of a tree" (122). As Matthias details the formidable alarm system, the others experience "a ripple of unease" (123) at the near impossibility of their task. Matthias guesses that Yul-Bayur will be in the White Island, beyond the ice moat, where the palace and treasury are located— "the most secure place in the Ice Court" (124), and the most difficult for foreigners to penetrate.

Nina points out that it's only two weeks till Hringkälla, or the Day of Listening, when new *drüskulle* are welcomed with a huge celebration on the White Island. Kaz decides to use Hringkälla as a distraction while his crew enters through the prison. They will enter as criminals, using the prison as their front door. Once incarcerated, they'll break out of the prison and exit through the embassy; with Hringkälla in full swing, they can pass unnoticed. Kaz assures the team that Yul-Bayur will trust them, since they have the code word established by the Merchant Council in earlier communication with the scientist: "*Sesh-uyeh,*" or "heartsick."

Chapter 9 Summary

Kaz tells the others to prepare to leave by ship the following night. He worries about Wylan and his wealthy background— "like a silk-eared puppy in a room full of fighting dogs" (130)—but he must keep the boy around to ensure Van Eck pays their reward. Kaz asks Jesper to watch out for Wylan, to Jesper's annoyance.

Matthias asks Kaz if they can speak alone and immediately attacks him, looking for the piece of paper with his pardon. The feeling of Matthias's bare skin on Kaz's "set[s] off a riot of revulsion in Kaz's head" (132), but Kaz quickly gains the upper hand. Kaz warns Matthias not to test him again.

Chapter 10 Summary

When Inej shares her doubts about their mission and Kaz's arrogance, Kaz reminds her she can be replaced. Inej wonders why she doesn't just walk away, and she remembers the Suli saying her father often told her: "The heart is an arrow. It demands aim to land true" (135). She knows she must be clear on her mission, yet she's still not sure what she wants. For now, she'll "settle for an apology" (136).

Running errands for Kaz, Inej passes the Menagerie where she was once indentured. She also passes a brothel called the House of Exotics, which is built "like a tiered cage" (137). The foreign girls who work there go by animal names; as a Suli, Inej was the lynx. Suddenly, the proprietor of the Menagerie—Heleen Van Houden, known as the Peacock to the public and as Tante Heleen to the Menagerie girls—grabs Inej by the arm. Hellen tells Inej, "You'll wear my silks again, I promise" (139), before letting her go. Inej touches her daggers, all named after Suli saints, and asks for protection.

Inej makes it to the dock where the crew waits by the schooner Kaz has commandeered, which is decked out like a Kerch hunters' ship. Then, the boat explodes.

Chapters 1-10 Analysis

When writing *Six of Crows,* Bardugo was inspired by the movie *Ocean's Eleven* and wanted to create a magical heist story. The opening chapters set up the ensemble cast, explain their impossible mission, and paint the magical world that surrounds them.

Although most of *Six of* Crow's protagonists come from the Barrel, a seedy and violent criminal district, the book opens in the wealthy merchant district of Ketterdam, home to equally dark and immoral activities. The Grisha, the world's magical element, possess powers to control the human body, physical objects, or the natural world. Their power is in danger of being co-opted for evil purposes thanks to the dangerous new drug *jurda parem*. Using the point of view of a guard who never appears again in the novel, Bardugo shows what happens to those who are under the control of a Grisha who's taken *jurda parem*.

Beginning with the second chapter, the novel alternates point of view between five of the protagonists, with each chapter told in the close third person point of view. Chapter 2 features Inej's perspective but serves above all to introduce Kaz, a teenage criminal mastermind and the central figure in the novel. Through Inej's eyes, readers observe how Kaz uses information he's gained by spying and trickery to orchestrate an encounter between rival gangs so it turns entirely in his favor. Kaz deals ruthlessly with the enemy gang's leader, his own soldier who has betrayed him, and even an innocent used as collateral—the rival's girlfriend, whom Kaz threatens to burn to death.

The chapter establishes the novel's theme of monstrosity, and also develops the violent world that causes characters to lose their humanity and become monsters: While Inej pities the hemorrhaging Dregs soldier, she doesn't save him. She thinks of her own gang identity as a ghost who spies and moves unseen, sneaking up on her enemies. She is the Wraith who has no time for traitors. Meanwhile, Kaz transforms himself into the merciless monster encapsulated by his gang name, Dirtyhands.

If Chapter 2 establishes Kaz's impenetrable public image, subsequent chapters hint at his secret vulnerabilities and construct the novel's plot. After the encounter with the rival gang, Kaz is kidnapped—something only possible through the powers of a Grisha under the influence of *jurda parem*—and offered the chance to complete a dangerous mission in exchange for an outrageous sum of money. Kaz's motivation for taking the mission—he thinks the money will allow him to take revenge on Pekka Rollins and quiet the voice of his brother's ghost—reveals both the loss that haunts him and vengeance as his motivating force. The high price of *jurda parem*—individually for Grisha who pursue the addiction even to their deaths, and broadly, for people who will suffer when governments who control the Grisha use them to start wars—cements the drug as a symbol of both greed and power.

In the remainder of the opening chapters, Kaz gathers the perfect crew for his heist. Two characters, Nina and Matthias, have opposing motivations that foreshadow significant conflict. Nina, a Grisha, has spent the past year in Ketterdam trying to get Matthias out of prison, even though he's a Fjerdan *drüskelle* who hunts Grisha. Kaz agrees to break Matthias out if Nina will join his crew, but when they retrieve Matthias, Nina finds him turned cold, "stripped of anything human" (93), after his year in the violent Hellsgate. What's more, Matthias considers Nina— and other Grisha—a *"traitor, witch, abomination"* (105). As a *drüskelle*, Matthias sees Grisha as monstrous beings whose magical powers go against the natural order; his viewpoints add another dimension to the theme of monstrosity in the novel.

Another critical theme that emerges is the search and desire for home. Despite Matthias's hatred for Nina and loyalty to his homeland, Kaz manages to lure Matthias to his cause by promising him a pardon that will allow him to return to Fjerda; Nina also wants to return to her homeland in Ravka. Nina and Matthias share a complex and thorny history, which is revealed in later chapters. Their bickering becomes a constant source of tension in the narrative.

The opening chapters also include Jesper's point of view without revealing his full motivation for joining Kaz's mission. Jesper has a restless nature and a weakness for gambling; his thoughts begin "buzzing and jumping at the possibility" of a large financial reward (121). Jesper also takes more of an interest in the sixth member of Kaz's crew, Wylan, than the rest of the group. Jesper teases Wylan for his inexperience and his coddled upbringing; until a few months earlier, Wylan was safe and comfortable in "daddy's mansion." Why Wylan left his rich merchant family to live in the Barrel remains a mystery. Kaz orders Jesper to keep an eye on Wylan, and Jesper seems annoyed at first, but in the end, the two will develop a strong relationship.

In Chapter 10, Inej's haunted past and her own motivations for helping Kaz become clearer. Forced into prostitution at the Menagerie, a brothel specializing in "exotic" girls like Inej, who has Suli heritage, she now works for the Dregs instead, spying for Kaz. She can't help caring for Kaz, even though he's told her she can be easily replaced. At the same time, Inej holds onto the heritage and family she's been torn away from: She remembers her father telling her, "The heart is an arrow. It demands aim to land true" (135). Not yet sure where to aim her heart, Inej goes along with Kaz's goals for the moment. Both her search for a deeper purpose and her attraction to Kaz, even as she's frustrated by his lack of empathy, develop further as the novel continues.

Chapters 11-20

Chapter 11 Summary

After the boat's explosion, Jesper stands in the midst of a gunfight, savoring the thrill of combat he first discovered on the Zemeni frontier alongside his father. He notices Wylan "curled up on the dock" (143) and pulls him up, forcing him to shoot. Kaz tells them to go to the next dock, where the real schooner is waiting; the boat that just exploded was a decoy. Kaz had anticipated other teams wanting to go after Yul-Bayer and knew they would ambush his crew.

Jesper sees Nina fighting the attackers with her Grisha powers. She frees Matthias, who is bound beside her, and gives him a pistol to join in the fight. Running through gunfire, Jesper and Wylan get to the real schooner, the *Ferolind,* first. Jesper orders a terrified Wylan to hold off the assailants while he heads for the crow's nest, though he's shot in the thigh on the way. Despite the painful injury, he picks off enemies from high in the sails, reminding himself how badly he needs the money to pay off his gambling debts.

Wylan yells for Jesper to close his eyes, and when Jesper opens them again, he realizes Wylan has set off a flash bomb. Jesper concludes the play was "not bad for a mercher's kid" (147).

Chapter 12 Summary

When the firefight breaks out on the docks, Inej climbs high onto the cargo crates, then slides down to take out one enemy after another with her daggers. She notices their attackers come from both the Black Tips and Razorgulls and wonders how many gangs they're fighting against.

Oomen, the Black Tips' enforcer, appears out of nowhere and stabs Inej under her arm. She jams one of her kneepads in his crotch, and he lets go of her; she's hidden tiny steel blades in both pads. Weak from blood loss, she hears her father saying, "Climb, Inej," just as he did when she was a child, and he taught her to perform as an acrobat. She can't make it high enough, and as she prepares to stab herself in the heart rather than be captured by the Black Tips, Kaz appears, plucks her up, and carries her toward the schooner.

Inej remembers first seeing Kaz at the Menagerie, where he paid Tante Heleen for intel about her clients. Inej told Kaz she could help him, and he returned the next day to take her away from the Menagerie. Now, he's come back for her again, but when she says so aloud, he claims he's only "protect[ing] my investments" (153). Inej demands an apology but blacks out before she can hear his answer.

Chapter 13 Summary

Kaz struggles on board with Inej in his arms, the pain in his leg "the worst it [has] been since he'd first broken it falling off [a] roof" (154). He orders his chosen captain, Specht, to set sail, then rushes below deck to Nina and commands her to heal Inej. He wonders what transgression Inej wanted an apology for— "there were so many possibilities" (156)—as he leaves Nina alone to work.

Jesper and Matthias grab Oomen, who was forced on board by one of Kaz's men. Kaz asks Oomen why the Black Tips are "out in force" (157) and yanks out Oomen's eyeball with his bare hand, threatening to take the other if he doesn't talk. Oomen admits that Pekka Rollins hired the

Black Tips to ambush the Dregs. Kaz wonders if Pekka is leading his own crew to the Ice Court, but Oomen knows nothing more, so Kaz throws him overboard. Kaz reflects that "it always came back to Pekka Rollins, the man who had taken everything from him" (206), and he feels determined to make Pekka suffer.

Chapter 14 Summary

Nina, a Heartrender Grisha and not a Healer, finds it difficult to save Inej. Nina wishes she'd had a more complete education, but Ravka's civil war cut her schooling short. She closes Inej's wound—all she can do for the moment—and observes that Inej has a partially removed tattoo of the Menagerie and no new Dregs tattoo. Nina has both a White Rose and a Dregs tattoo: "a crow trying to drink from a near empty goblet" (162). The tattoo signaled to others that "to trifle with [Nina] was to risk [the Dregs'] vengeance" (162).

Nina joined the Grisha's Second Army following the Ravkan civil war. After a particularly harsh scolding from a superior, she wandered off and ended up in a *drüskelle* camp, where she was captured by a *drüskelle* with hair of "burnished gold"—Matthias—and thrown on a ship with other Grisha prisoners.

One day the *drüskelle* leader Jarl Brum, whom the Grisha whisper about as a "monster waiting in the dark" (168), addressed the prisoners, telling them they would be tried and executed. One *drüskelle* reached for Nina and wondered if he could have some fun with her, but Matthias—whose name Nina didn't know at the time—smacked the other man and asked, "Would you fornicate with a dog?" (170). The other *drüskelle* left and Nina, drawing on her talent for languages, asked Matthias in

Fjerdan of what crimes the *drüskelle* accused her. Matthias refused to elaborate, and she asked him for water. He brought back a tin cup and bucket of water; later, Nina recalls "that tin cup had saved her life" (171).

Nina falls asleep and wakes to find Inej alive and stable. Matthias watches her from the doorway. They trade barbs, and Matthias wonders why Kaz asked Nina about the White Rose. Nina shows Matthias her White Rose tattoo, and he asks why she worked there and stayed in Kerch. Nina says she was trying "to set things right" (174) and free Matthias from prison, but he doesn't believe her. Nina studies Matthias, remembering the good things she once saw inside him after the shipwreck, and wonders if the goodness survived his stint in prison.

Chapter 15 Summary

Back on deck, Matthias thinks of Nina, telling him she'd made a mistake by branding him a slaver and having him jailed, but he's still sure a Grisha has no honor. Kaz gives his crew an invention called *baleen*, a disc that can be used for breathing underwater if bitten down on while a person is drowning. Matthias fills in place names on the map Wylan drew of the Ice Court, an act that makes Matthias feel "even more treasonous" (178). He wonders if, after being assumed dead in the shipwreck that killed his fellow *drüskelle* and Commander Brum, he could turn in the Dregs and return to the Fjerdans' good graces.

Kaz asks Matthias about the prison layout and develops a plan for Inej to climb out through the incinerator. Jesper brings up the bigger problem of Pekka Rollins: Competing with Pekka over this mission will incite a gang war. Kaz insists that if the Dregs pull off this job first, they'll become bigger legends than Pekka. Jesper about what his ghost will do "if Pekka Rollins kills us all" (181).

Chapter 16 Summary

After three days at sea, Inej wakes after midnight feeling "sore, but not terrible" (186). Nina catches Inej up on the outcome of the fight, and Inej asks Nina to stay while she rests. Nina asks Inej why she doesn't have a Dregs tattoo, and Inej points out the scars left behind from her Menagerie tattoo. Desperate to remove the brothel's mark, she paid for a hack job that left "a puckered spill of wounds" (187). Inej didn't want to be marked again, even by the Dregs. Yet in a way, Inej thinks, she has been marked by Kaz. She cares for him despite her attempts to keep from becoming emotionally vulnerable.

Inej still can't sleep, and she and Nina connect over the fact that both associate boats with bad memories. As Nina sings to Inej, Inej remembers herself at 14. She and her family lived in a Suli caravan and performed in a carnival by the sea. One morning, she'd remained in her family's wagon alone for a few extra minutes of sleep when slavers arrived and kidnapped her. She was imprisoned in a ship's hold, along with other children. When she arrived in Kerch, she was handed over to Tante Heleen, who recognized the value in Inej's flawless, golden-brown Suli skin.

Chapter 17 Summary

With six days until the ship arrives in northern Fjerda, Jesper feels antsy enough to "hurl himself overboard" (192). He checks on Inej every day and eventually finds her well enough to rise, although Jesper has to help her walk to the deck. The crew members thank Inej for defeating the

Black Tips and wish her well. As Jesper observes, "it's a novelty to feel appreciated" (197).

Inej asks if Kaz came to check on her, and Jesper admits he didn't, but speculates it would have been difficult for Kaz to see her in that condition. Jesper asks Inej about Wylan's past, and Inej shares what little she knows from her investigations. Wylan appeared in the Barrel three months ago, using a fake name; according to rumor, Wylan was "caught in a sweaty romp" with a tutor (198). Councilman Van Eck sent Wylan letters every week, asking him to return home, but Wylan didn't open them. Jesper concludes Van Eck must have done something terrible to make Wylan "slum it with us" (199).

Inej wonders why Jesper has taken on this dangerous mission, and he admits he's in debt to his own father, whose farm in Novyi Zem has just started to make a profit. Jesper's father loaned Jesper money he believes is for university, but it's actually to pay off gambling debts. Jesper needs to pay his father back, and this job is the only way.

Chapter 18 Summary

Two days after Inej is back on her feet, Kaz finally "make[s] himself approach" her (202). He shows her the map of the Ice Court, and she agrees she can climb the incinerator shaft. Kaz recalls snapping at Inej before they began the mission, and he now knows she was echoing his own worries. Now, he needs Inej to believe in him so he can have the confidence to continue.

Inej mentions Pekka Rollins, and Kaz reveals that Pekka killed his brother. Inej promises to pray Kaz's brother will have "peace in the next world" (204). Kaz is surprised his skin isn't crawling at his nearness to Inej; he actually wants to move closer. Inej asks Kaz what he wants from the mission, and he claims he simply wants money. He asks Inej about her goals, and she says she wants to leave Ketterdam and never hear the name Wraith again. Kaz leaves frustrated with Inej, and he starts to think of his childhood.

When Kaz was nine, his father was crushed by a plow, and Jordie sold the family farm and took his brother to Ketterdam. The boys rented a room in a boardinghouse, and every morning, Jordie ordered Kaz to stay inside, left to look for work, and returned home disappointed. One night, Kaz convinced Jordie to take him to East Stave, where they'd seen a performing magician. The boys passed Pekka's Emerald Palace and at the next gambling hall, the Golden Strike, Kaz stopped to play with the little wind-up dogs for sale out front. The boy selling the dogs, Filip, told Jordie about a job as a runner, and he invited Jordie to come back the next day so they could ask about the job together.

The next day, Filip and Jordie both found jobs running messages for Jacob Hertzoon, a coffeehouse owner who arranged investment deals for trade ships. Kaz spent his days at the coffeehouse, and the boys even shared dinner with the Hertzoons. Overhearing information about the trade deals, Kaz realized Hertzoon's associates were using inside knowledge to cheat in their investments. Jordie decided to invest his father's money in one of those deals—the moment, Kaz now realizes, when "greed [took] hold of his brother" (210).

A week later, Jordie and Kaz discovered the coffeehouse closed and the Hertzoon residence abandoned. A neighbor told them the Hertzoons had only rented the house for a few weeks. Jordie held out hope the Hertzoons would return, but Kaz remembered the magician's coin that had fascinated him so—like Jordie's money, it was "there and then gone" (212).

Chapter 19 Summary

The *Ferolind* arrives on the northern coast of Fjerda, and Kaz sends Nina to unlock Matthias's shackles before they disembark. Kaz also wants Nina to "tailor" Matthias—to use her Grisha abilities to make him look different, so he won't be recognizable. She darkens his hair, and Matthias struggles for composure as her lips draw so close to his that "if he sat up straighter, they'd be kissing" (216). Before she leaves, Nina tells Matthias she doesn't "believe for a second" (217) he'll allow the Dregs to deliver Yul-Bayur to the Kerch merchants.

The crew departs the ship, and the captain Specht says he'll pick them up in Djerholm harbor once the mission is complete. The ship is their escape route, as it carries papers that claim they're transporting goods from Fjerda back to Kerch. They spend a day hiking toward civilization, and Matthias is a little pleased to see the others struggling in the cold to which he's accustomed— "the white north had a way of forcing strangers to reevaluate their terms" (218).

The next day, Kaz begins to go over the plan. The crew will be taken to holding cells before being charged. After completing a few tasks in the prison, they'll climb rope placed by Inej in the incinerator shaft and cross to the embassy roof, thus avoiding the embassy checkpoints. Jesper will watch out for Wylan and help him make bombs from prison supplies, which will only be used if necessary. Matthias, hearing the plan, secretly considers killing Yul-Bayur at some point.

As the group continues traveling, Matthias remembers the shipwreck that transformed his life—a shipwreck that occurred only miles from where the team landed. When the storm tossed the *drüskelles'* ship "like a toy" and "dragged [it] under" (224), Nina somehow escaped her shackles and rescued Matthias, using magic to keep him alive and pulling him along with her. Eventually, Matthias began swimming, and Nina's powers "kept both of them breathing" (225) until they found land. Matthias considered abandoning Nina, but she'd saved his life— "a blood debt" (227)—so he guided her back toward civilization. Along the way, they got to know each other: psychologically, as Matthias bristled against Nina's brash, immodest words and actions; and physically, as they lay close to each other at night to stay warm. Matthias must admit that he's attracted to Nina, that he truly "did like the way she talked" (230)— and still does.

The crew comes across a pyre with tree stakes and the charred bodies of Grisha. "This is what Fjerdans do to Grisha" (231), Nina says, although Matthias insists the pyres are now illegal. They realize one of the girls is still alive, and Jesper shoots her to put her out of her misery. As Matthias and Nina argue over the Fjerdans treatment of Grisha, Matthias reveals that Grisha soldiers burned his entire village, killing his parents and sister.

Chapter 20 Summary

Despite Matthias's hatred of Grisha, Nine can't change the fact that "one smile from Matthias Helvar [felt] like 50 from someone else" (234). She thinks back to the three weeks they spent wandering after the shipwreck. No matter how separate they kept themselves as they fell asleep, in the morning they'd wake "pressed together, breathing in tandem […] a single crescent moon" (235). Nina revealed how she used the jagged lip of the tin cup Matthias brought her to cut the Grisha's bonds; they planned to attack the *drüskelle,* but the storm changed their plans. In spite of their mutual distrust, Nina and Matthias developed an ever-strengthening bond, their insults becoming increasingly playful and flirtatious until Matthias admitted he liked Nina. The two became "Nina and Matthias instead of Grisha and witchhunter" (241)—but now, Nina considers the intimacy of those weeks a lie.

In the present, Nina and Matthias continue tussling, both verbally and physically, until the others order them to stop fighting or they'll "get us all killed" (242). Matthias forces Nina to admit what she did: When the two reached a town after the shipwreck, Matthias kept Nina's identity hidden and began to arrange transport to Kerch, but Nina told the Kerch that Matthias was a slaver who'd captured her. The Kerch "tossed [Matthias] in the brig" (244) until they reached Ketterdam, and he ended up in Hellsgate. Now, Matthias asks Nina if she would undo her actions, and she insists she'd "do it all over again" (244).

Suddenly the earth erupts beneath the crew's feet, and Nina realizes they're being attacked by Grisha Squallers flying above them—something only possible with the aid of *jurda parem.* The Grisha are shooting slabs of rock and ice in a circle around the group, trying to trap them. Wylan sets off a bomb as a distraction, and Jesper shoots one of the Grisha down while Inej attacks the other. Wylan sets a larger bomb to destroy the slabs that have entrapped them. Nina recognizes the Grisha boy wounded by both Inej's knife and Jesper's bullet; he's Nestor, one of her schoolmates. Nestor begs desperately for more *jurda parem* and for the Shu to come back, and then he collapses, dead, his body "ravaged by the drug" (247).

Kaz finds a Shu *wen ye,* or "Coin of Passage" (248), in the other Grisha's pocket and surmises the Grisha were sent by the Shu government to collect Yul-Bayur. Nina wonders why they need the scientist if they already have *jurda parem,* and Kaz guesses that either only Yul-Bayur knows how to make more of the drug, or they want to ensure he doesn't share the formula. He expects more drugged, dangerous Grisha are heading for the Ice Court.

Nina wants to bury the Grisha, and Matthias agrees to help her while the rest of the team continues moving—Nina and Matthias will catch up later. As they dig the graves, Nina wonders if what she saw in the influence of *jurda parem* is what Fjerdans see in all Grisha: an abomination, "the natural world undone" (251). Matthias asks Nina why she turned him in as a slaver, and Nina reveals that Grisha saw her with Matthias and asked her to turn him in. She saw the Grisha coming to collect Matthias at the docks, and she accused him of being a slaver so the Kerch would take him away because she believed he'd be safer in Kerch than with the Grisha. Once in Ketterdam, she tried to recant her testimony, but no one would listen.

Matthias is sure Nina will attempt to kill Yul-Bayur in order to save the Grisha, and Nina and Matthias realize they both want the scientist dead, even if doing so "mean[s] betraying the others" (254). Just as they did after the shipwreck, the two establish an uneasy truce, a determination that "Bo Yul-Bayur will not leave the Ice Court alive" (254).

Chapters 11-20 Analysis

These chapters begin with the Dregs fighting off an ambush meant to destroy their ship, with Inej seriously injured in the process. The crew learns that Pekka Rollins ordered the ambush, and Kaz surmises Pekka is heading to the Ice Court himself, also bent on retrieving Yul-Bayur. Immediately, Kaz homes in on his desire to avenge his brother, again highlighting revenge as a primary motivation driving his behavior. The fight indicates how dangerous their mission will be, foreshadowing more dire situations to follow.

As Kaz rescues Inej and carries her to the ship, Inej recalls him rescuing her in a different way from the Menagerie, when he bought her indenture and brought her to work for the Dregs. Inej longs for Kaz to care for her emotionally in the same way he does physically. When he claims he is only protecting his investments, Inej wonders whether he's telling the truth or bluffing to hide deeper feelings. Kaz feels physically drawn to Inej, even though the touch of human skin rouses feelings of revulsion in him; in Chapter 9, he is repulsed by the touch of Matthias's skin on his. Later chapters will reveal the reason why Kaz reacts so negatively to physical touch and why his desire for Inej's touch is so significant.

Once the ship leaves Ketterdam for Fjerda, the crew members forge new connections and reveal formative incidents from their past. As Nina uses her Grisha powers to tend to the wounded Inej, the two young women bond over being ripped from their homelands. Shared memories between two other character, Nina and Matthias, cause both to question their definitions of "monster." Nina thinks of the *drüskelle* leader Jarl Brum as a "monster waiting in the dark" (168) who cruelly hunts down Grisha; Matthias reveals that Grisha burned his village and killed his family. For him, the Grisha are the monsters while Brum is a hero. Monstrosity is a matter of perspective.

Jesper is by far the most antsy of the characters on the ship, "hoping they'd be attacked by pirates" (192) just so he can experience the excitement of another fight. Jesper has an unusually restless nature, which he attempts to appease by annoying Wylan. The two forge a friendship based on trading barbs, although Wylan's reasons for joining the Dregs remain a mystery. Jesper's own motivations become clearer when he visits a recovering Inej and admits he's borrowed money from his father to pay gambling debts, so he desperately needs the reward money to pay his father back. Jesper is clearly haunted by the fact he "can never walk away from a bad hand" (200), even when his gambling compulsion threatens the home he's left but still loves.

Unlike the other characters, Kaz waits to visit Inej until she's recovered from her injury. Although he seems indifferent to her, inwardly he "need[s] to know that [Inej] believed he could do this" (204). Kaz surprises himself by sharing a secret with Inej he hasn't told anyone else: He tells her Pekka killed his brother. The conversation reveals how Kaz, like the other characters, lost both his home and his family. Although the full story isn't yet revealed, readers begin to understand how Kaz has become so hardened and suspicious at such a young age. The merchant who duped Jordie reminds Kaz of a "magician's coin: there and then gone" (212); over time, magic tricks become an important motif in the novel. Kaz's experience has motivated him to become the magician rather than the one being tricked.

Chapters 19 and 20 incorporate Matthias and Nina's points of view as the crew lands in Fjerda and treks through the cold countryside—a trip Matthias and Nina have taken together before. Despite the fact that the Grisha and *drüskelle* each consider the other side monstrous, during their search for rescue in Fjerda, Nina and Matthias grew to care for each other as individuals. They became "Nina and Matthias instead of Grisha and witchhunter" (241), another example of the novel's message that monstrosity and humanity depend on perspective.

Matthias has great difficulty believing Nina didn't truly betray him, and their dance of attraction and anger reaches a turning point. When the two share a moment alone, Nina realizes they might once again be "allies instead of enemies" (254), as neither of them wants Yul-Bayur to live and pass on the secret of *jurda parem*. Nina hopes to keep the Grisha safe, while Matthias doesn't want to betray the Fjerdans holding Yul-Bayur captive, and they make a pact to go against the rest of the Dregs by ensuring "Bo Yul-Bayur will not leave the Ice Court alive" (254). The mechanics of the novel's heist structure have suddenly become more complex, with characters secretly working toward opposing goals, and the trickery foreshadows more danger and complications to come.

Chapters 21-34

Chapter 21 Summary

Two days pass before the crew reaches the cliffs over Djerholm, where the Ice Court stands "like a great white sentinel" (258) and the town is busy with Hringkälla celebrations. The group observes the prison wagon and decides they'll use a "bunk biscuit" tactic, replacing six prisoners with themselves to get inside the Court.

The team finds a place to camp and wait for the next morning's wagon. Inej sleeps until midday, so tired she's "close to collapse" (266), and still suffering the effects of her injury. Wylan uses a chemical to down a tree across the

road, which will force the wagon to stop. While the driver
and guard deal with the tree, Kaz picks the lock on the
wagon but then freezes, his face "pale, almost waxen" as he
sees the prisoners "tightly packed together" with black bags
over their heads (269). Finally, Kaz manages to move,
clearly shaken as he unlocks the prisoners' shackles.

Kaz and Inej lead six prisoners away, and Nina spells them
into unconsciousness. The crew enters the wagon and they
place shackles and hoods on each other, while Inej locks
the wagon from the outside, then enters through the other
side of the door where Kaz has removed the hinges. Once
they're all inside, Inej realizes Kaz is still agitated and
working slowly, but finally the guards return and drive the
wagon forward without checking inside. Then Kaz,
breathing "like an animal caught in a trap" (272), faints.

Chapter 22 Summary

Kaz remembers his time in Ketterdam with Jordie. The
money from Hertzoon ran out, and when Jordie brought the
loan agreement between himself and Hertzoon to the bank,
they discovered it was "worthless paper" and no one had
heard of Hertzoon. Thrown out of the boardinghouse, they
spent a few nights on the streets before both fell victim to
the firepox outbreak. They lay together in "a pile of
broken-up wooden boxes" until Jordie died and his body
turned "cold and hard" (274).

Both Jordie and Kaz were collected on a sickboat and
dumped in Reaper's Barge, where Kaz dreamed of happy
memories with Jordie and woke with his brother's body
beside him, "swollen with rot […] like some kind of
gruesome deep sea fish" (275). Kaz's own fever passed, but
he wondered if he should simply give up; then he realized
"vengeance for Jordie and maybe for himself, too" awaited

back on land (276). Kaz used his brother's body as a raft to guide himself back to land and then let Jordie's body float away. Kaz knew he must live, for "someone had to pay" (276).

Kaz wakes in the prison wagon, where Inej tells him they've passed the first two checkpoints. The wagon stops and opens, and the prisoners are led forward, their hoods ripped off. They find themselves in a courtyard where guards confirm each prisoner is on the driver's list. Kaz is surprised to find the Ice Court a "dreamlike" place "so white it almost glow[s] blue" (278), a place Nina comments must be the work of Fabrikator Grisha. Nina points out five bodies impaled on spikes over the courtyard, including one with a Dime Lion tattoo. Kaz wonders if one of the other bodies belongs to Rollins, but hopes none do—in Kaz's mind, Pekka Rollins and his death "belong […] to him" (279).

The guards fuss over the disparity between the driver's paperwork and Kaz's team, but they decide to take them into the prison and "let the next shift sort them out" (280). The prisoners separate into male and female groups, and each must be touched by a "human amplifier"—a person who can detect Grisha by touch. The amplifier lets Nina pass, either because of the paraffin in which they'd coated Nina's arm, or because the woman simply let her go. Kaz has a moment of panic as Inej is led away from him; he relied on her as the one who "brought him back from the dark" after the episode on the wagon (281).

The male prisoners are taken to a room with hoses, where they're forced to strip down. The task brings Kaz back to the "bodies crowding around him" in the sickboat (282), and he nearly faints again but manages to stay conscious, though a guard discovers the two lockpicks hidden in his mouth. After being hosed down, the prisoners are given uniforms and deposited in holding cells of "dank gray rock and iron bars" (284), where Kaz's ungloved hands feel impossibly bare and, without his cane, he must limp.

Chapter 23 Summary

In the prison, Jesper struggles to contain his restless energy, the same energy that drove him from his father's farm to Ketterdam, where he'd hoped to find direction at the university but ended up consumed by gambling and gang warfare. As they wait, Jesper tries to coax a terrified Wylan to share more about his past, but Wylan reveals only that his father took him everywhere until something significant changed.

When a guard brings water, Jesper gets himself and Wylan wet, then opens the stitches on his ankle and pulls out a pellet Nina had buried inside him. He warns the crew to pull their shirts over their heads, then puts the pellet in a waste bucket, emitting a chloro gas that causes the other prisoners to pass out. Jesper goes to the prison bars and manages to pull iron from it; as Matthias observes, Jesper is actually a Fabrikator Grisha, if a weak one. Jesper pulls two slim needles of iron from the bars, and Kaz uses them to pick the locks. The crew splits up to complete their assignments.

Jesper and Matthias run to the stables, grab rope, and head to the rendezvous point in the basement. Wylan and Inej enter the trash room, where they discover a problem: The incinerator now runs in the afternoon rather than in the morning. The team cannot carry explosives above the still-smoldering coals, and they're not sure if they can climb the shaft at all. Kaz and Nina have already left to search the prison for Yul-Bayur, just in case he's somewhere inside, even though they were supposed to wait for Jesper and Matthias to accompany them. Wylan finds Inej's leather shoes discarded in the laundry. With the help of those "magic slippers," Inej feels sure she can make the climb.

Chapter 24 Summary

Nina wonders why Kaz has insisted he and Nina climb the upper floors of the prison alone as they dodge guards, searching through the prisoners and finding no Shu among them. Nina passes through a steel door to a strange room with walls of "white so clean it hurt to look at" and one wall half of glass, which must be "Fabrikator made" (297). Through the glass, she sees cells of the same brilliant white, a floor drain "surrounded by reddish stains" (297), and only one item: a button with the insignia of a Grisha Squaller. She surmises that Grisha slaves had constructed this trap for Grisha prisoners, creating a place their magic would not allow them to escape.

Horrified by what she's seen and yearning to return home, Nina rushes back to the meeting spot but doesn't see Kaz. She returns to the basement, using her powers to break the neck of a guard who intercepts her, and then the Elderclock sounds with a "shrill clamor": an alarm.

Chapter 25 Summary

Wearing Kaz's gloves retrieved from the laundry—she can't touch the incinerator walls with bare skin—Inej holds heavy ropes and scales six stories with "the fires of hell burning below" (301). She struggles, the bricks so hot her shoes literally melt, slipping as she realizes "there was no one to save her" (303).

Inej remembers the night Kaz came to collect her from the Menagerie. The Dregs' boss, Per Haskell, had bought Inej's indenture. Kaz explained that Haskell's contract, unlike Tante Heleen's, will eventually allow Inej to pay off her debts and become free; he doesn't promise her safety or happiness. Inej prefers his "terrible truths" to "kind lies" and accepts his offer.

Now, in the incinerator shaft, Inej blames herself for trusting Kaz, allowing him to "lead her to this fate" (309). Inej can't return home after the shame of working at the Menagerie and killing for the Dregs, and she considers giving up—but she can't abandon the others who are relying on her. Suddenly she feels raindrops, cooling the walls and her melting shoes. Her strength renewed, she climbs quickly while imagining a storm, a future in which she seeks revenge and "hunt[s] the slavers and their buyers" (311).

Chapter 26 Summary

Kaz rushes through the prison, searching for Pekka Rollins, feeling "like a wild animal" (312), as he did after Jordie's death. He remembers his first days alone, how the firepox and Jordie's demise "burned away every gentle thing inside him" (313). Kaz slashed the feet of a young boy working at a gambling house in order to take his job, and while cleaning for the gambling house, he learned how to steal and fight. Discarding his family's surname, Rietveld, "like a rotten limb" (314), Kaz took the name Brekker from a piece of machinery so he wouldn't be recognizable to Jakob Hertzoon.

At the gambling house, Kaz learned that Hertzoon's con was a frequent tactic in the Barrel. Kaz also discovered his own "gift for cards" (315) and was soon banned from play from every gambling house. One day Kaz saw a man he recognized as Hertzoon, with his "florid cheeks and tufty sideburns" (315) and followed him to a gin shop where the guard wouldn't let Kaz inside. The guard told Kaz the man wasn't Hertzoon, but Pekka Rollins, a legendary Barrel gang boss. Rollins looked through the shop window, right at Kaz, and didn't appear to remember the boy.

That evening, Kaz realized if he wanted to take everything from Pekka, he needed the strength of a gang behind him. The next day, he asked Per Haskell if he could work for the Dregs. Though Kaz began as a "grunt," he knew "the Dregs would become his army" (316).

Now, in the Ice Court prison, Kaz finally finds Pekka's florid face. Asleep in his cell, Pekka has recently received a bad beating. Kaz picks the lock and enters the cell to find Pekka smiling; he was faking sleep. Pekka asks if Kaz has come to gloat, and Kaz lets the cell door close.

Chapter 27 Summary

As the alarm blares and boots stomp above, Jesper wonders where Kaz has gone. Inej has made it to the roof and dropped rope for Wylan, Matthias, and Nina to climb, and now Jesper waits for Kaz, alone in the basement. Finally, Kaz bursts in, his clothing covered in blood, and Jesper begins to climb with Kaz behind him.

They find Matthias and Wylan on the roof, while Inej and Nina have already moved on to the embassy. The four use the rope and a sliding sling Inej has constructed to transfer to the lower embassy roof, where Nina and Inej hide against a skylight dome. Nina tries to heal Inej's burned feet and orders Jesper to help her, thus revealing his Fabrikator status to the entire crew.

The crew demands an explanation for Kaz's disappearance, and he admits he was searching for Pekka, but claims he couldn't locate the man. On the White Island below, the crew sees guards organizing partygoers, creating another checkpoint before the glass bridge, likely a precaution after the prison alarm. Inej notices girls from the Ketterdam brothels have arrived for the celebration, and she knows how she and Nina will get through the checkpoint: they'll "enter with the Menagerie" (327).

Chapter 28 Summary

Kaz points out that there must be another route to the White Island besides the bridge, and Matthias admits he knows of one, but it's "messy." Kaz asks Wylan if he can disable one of the embassy gates and keep it shut to trigger Black Protocol—the highest state of emergency—which will cause the bridge to close and trap the guards on White Island.

Inej and Nina disguise themselves as members of the Menagerie, using Grisha magic to create tattoos. The entire crew shares a moment before they depart for their missions, knowing they might not make it out alive. They all repeat the Dregs' motto: "no mourners" and "no funerals" (332). Inej pulls Kaz aside and gives him his gloves, recovered from the laundry. Then she tells them after the heist, she's leaving the Dregs. Kaz starts to speak, and Inej touches his cheek— "the first time she had touched him skin to skin" in their two years together (333). Kaz allows the touch but appears to be "waging a war with himself" (334)—not pulling back is "the best he [can] offer," but for Inej, it's "not enough" (334). She makes a last silent prayer for Kaz and leaves him, knowing her true purpose will lead her away from him.

Inej and Nina crawl through air ducts until they're above the room where the Menagerie girls are searched before entering the White Island. Nina uses magic to strip and bind the girls, taking the place of two of them and hiding the rest in a closet. Nina passes the guards' inspection, but Inej is flagged as suspicious and taken back to the checkpoint.

Chapter 29 Summary

Matthias, Kaz, Jesper, and Wylan cross a rope to the roof of the *drüskelle* building. Matthias feels at home here, but in his new status as invader, it's "home turned on its head" (343). Matthias admits that his feelings for Nina, and the relief he'd felt when she emerged alive from the incinerator, have overtaken his loyalty to the *drüskelle*. Kaz and Matthias rappel to the shores of the ice moat, leaving Jesper and Wylan behind, and Matthias locates the secret, partially submerged bridge across the moat, shared only with *drüskelle* initiates. The Dregs cover themselves with white powder from a wall, to hide themselves from the guards, and walk across the bridge as the icy waters soak their feet. Kaz picks the gate lock, and they enter the White Island near the guards' barracks.

Two guards pass, and Matthias knocks one unconscious with a rifle. He realizes Kaz is unarmed, and that he could shoot him and betray the Dregs, but he chooses not to—something Kaz affirms is a test. Matthias is no longer loyal to the *drüskelle* guards he once called brothers, and along with Kaz, he puts on a fallen guard's uniform, ready to continue the Dregs' mission.

Chapter 30 Summary

Jesper and Wylan cross the *drüskelle* roof to the gatehouse, Jesper drunk on the "adrenaline crackl[ing] through his body" (349). Through a glass skylight, Jesper sees a banner made of cloth in Grisha colors and realizes they're trophies of dead Grisha. His mood now sober, Jesper remembers his father urging him to hide his Grisha powers, for "the world can be cruel" to those who possess magic (351).

At the gatehouse, Jesper starts to rappel down to disable a single guard, but two more guards emerge while he dangles above them. Suddenly, Jesper hears a voice singing in Fjerdan; it's Wylan, impersonating a drunk and dancing on the gatehouse walkway. The guards laugh and sing as well, giving Jesper the advantage he needs to land on one and wring his neck. Wylan joins the fight, and they disable all three guards. Wylan explains he learned Fjerdan from his tutors, and Jesper is impressed.

Inside the gatehouse, Wylan is dismayed to see steel chains rather than rope controlling the gates. They will have to rely on Jesper's Grisha power to cut through the metal.

Chapter 31 Summary

Nina crosses the glass bridge with the rest of the Menagerie, disconcerted by the thought that the bridge must be "Fabrikator craft." She enters a palace that seems "hollowed out of a glacier" (358), arriving in a ballroom full of ice sculptures of wolves. Heading for a group of soldiers, she reasons that a military officer will know where Yul-Bayur is being kept. She steps into a soldier's path so that he'll trip her, and the nearby general will come to her rescue. The general appears interested in Nina, but then a nearby man makes a joke, and Nina turns to discover he's

Jarl Brum, the *drüskelle* leader she'd believed was "at the bottom of the ocean" (360).

Chapter 32 Summary

Jesper, using magic, and Wylan, using scissors, struggle to weaken one link of the gate chain. The task is taking too long and Jesper decides they'll instigate the Black Protocol, then "shoot at the winch until it gives up" (360). Wylan remarks on Jesper's love of guns, and Jesper asks what Wylan loves. Wylan responds with "music. Numbers. Equations" (362). Jesper comments, "If only you could talk to girls in equations" (362), and when Wylan asks if Jesper is only interested in girls, Jesper admits that he's not.

The two turn the winch, raising the gate and triggering the Black Protocol. They let go of the winch so the gate falls, but the weakened link still doesn't break. Finally, with both boys hanging on the chain like "crazed squirrels," the link breaks, and the gate can no longer open.

Chapter 33 Summary

Inej waits in the embassy entryway with other detainees. She makes a scene, demanding an escort to the embassy gate as part of her escape plan. Tante Heleen appears, exposing Inej as "the Wraith [...] one of the most notorious criminals in Ketterdam" (366). Heleen grabs Inej, demanding to know the location of the girl Inej replaced; Inej truly feels like "a wraith," a spirit "taking flight" from the body Heleen has beaten and sold to men.

Inej remembers her body has also "given her strength" (367), and she brutally twists Heleen's wrist before the guards pull her away. Suddenly the Black Protocol rings out, and the guards take Inej out a gate that seals shut behind them, while Inej is haunted by the echoes of Heleen's laughter.

Chapter 34 Summary

Nina flirts with Jarl Brum, hoping he doesn't recognize her in her costume, so different from the "filthy and frightened" (368) prisoner she was before. She pretends to be curious about seeing a Grisha in person, and he asks if she wants to see one that night. She agrees, and he leads her out of the palace to a building that resembles a tomb: the old treasure vault, he explains, which has since been "converted into a laboratory" (374). He leads her to cells where nearly 30 Grisha are imprisoned. Clearly dosed with *jurda parem*, the Grisha have hollow eyes and scratch at themselves. Still flirtatious, Nina says she wants to spend time with Jarl alone, hoping she can torture him and get him to reveal Yul-Bayur's location. Jarl tricks her into a cell, locks her inside, and states her name—he remembers her "stubborn little face" (377). He tells her if he presses a button outside the cell, it will send *jurda parem* gas into the cell. Then he disappears, and Matthias's face appears outside the cell door. He tells her he "came to warn Brum as soon as [he] could" (377), putting "country before self" (378).

Matthias tells Nina, "Now our debt is paid" (378), as the Black Protocol sounds.

Chapters 21-34 Analysis

As the crew breaks into the Ice Court and begins to enact their plan to retrieve Yul-Bayur, more of the protagonists' secrets and vulnerabilities come to light. Themes of monsters and revenge take shape, and characters find themselves face to face with figures from their pasts.

As the crew sneaks into the Ice Court on a prison wagon, Kaz's phobia of physical touch almost overcomes him. In his newly vulnerable state, Kaz admits how deeply he cares for Inej, as he relies on her support to bring him "back from the dark" (281). Kaz's experience has forced him to acknowledge the human beneath the impenetrable, monstrous Dirtyhands; unlike his gang persona, Kaz cares about and even needs other people. At the same time, Inej undergoes her own transformation. During a near-impossible climb up an incinerator shaft, she decides on a new purpose that gives her the strength to continue: She will hunt the slavers and their buyers who destroy the lives of girls like her. In a twist on the theme of vengeance, Inej finds an empowering use for revenge. Her quest for vengeance reveals a nobler side rather than a darker one.

Kaz wastes valuable time searching for Pekka in the prison, while simultaneously remembering the true meaning Pekka holds for him. Knowing that killing Pekka when he's already weak would not give Kaz the satisfaction he's dreamed of, Kaz leaves the task for later, foreshadowing a greater confrontation to come. While Inej uses her new purpose literally to carry her upward, Kaz's own thirst for vengeance nearly destroys the mission.

In a twist of the novel's theme of longing for home and belonging, Matthias finds he no longer belongs in the community of Grisha hunters. He thinks of "Inej's courage and Jesper's daring," and "Nina, always Nina" (343). Matthias has found a true sense of belonging among this group of outcasts, and when he has the chance to shoot Kaz, he doesn't. Instead, he reveals the *drüskelle's* secrets to the Dregs to help them escape, choosing his new family over his old one.

As Matthias lets go of a part of his identity, Jesper confronts a part of himself he's long kept hidden. When Jesper uses magic to manipulate metal so the Dregs can escape, the rest of the crew discovers he's a Fabrikator Grisha. As he moves through the Ice Court, Jesper sees signs of how the Grisha were persecuted in the place, and he remembers his own father urging him to hide his Grisha abilities. Now, Jesper must face the choice of whether to keep his powers hidden or to learn to use them as Nina does hers. At the same time, Jesper grows closer to Wylan in these chapters: Wylan saves Jesper from being shot by guards, and the two hint at a mutual attraction.

As the prison break unfolds, Nina and Inej impersonate members of the Menagerie brothel, and both girls confront frightening enemies. Inej is attacked by Heleen, the Menagerie owner who once beat and sold her, and who now reveals her as a criminal before the Ice Court guards. With the strength of her new purpose—to take down slavers—and her confidence in "a body that had given her strength" (367), Inej fights back against Heleen. Both literally and symbolically, Inej fights back against the exploitation she suffered in her past and works toward her new goals.

Nina must face her own nemesis: Jarl Brum, the "monster" who captured and planned to execute her. When she discovers Brum is a guest at the Ice Court, Nina hopes he doesn't recognize her and tries to trick him into revealing Yul-Bayur's location. She prepares to leave Brum "gasping for breath" (376), but before she can do so, Brum reveals he knows her true identity and imprisons her. Matthias appears, apparently on Brum's side. Unlike Inej, Nina has not yet overpowered the forces that threaten to destroy her, and her relationship with Matthias once again becomes her Achilles heel.

Chapters 35-46

Chapter 35 Summary

Matthias talks with Jarl, who explains the *drüskelle* use
jurda parem along with a sedative to control the Grisha.
Because they still haven't mastered the drug's formula,
they've allowed Yul-Bayur to live for "as long as he can be
of service" (380).
Matthias wonders how long this Grisha prison has been at
the White Palace, and Jarl tells him it's existed for 15
years. Grisha sentenced to death are not truly executed but
are imprisoned as the *drüskelle* attempt to control them;
with *jurda parem*, the *drüskelle* have finally achieved that
control. The Grisha, according to Jarl, are less than human:
They are "born to be weapons […] to serve the soldiers of
Djel" (381). Matthias questions whether Nina can truly be a
monster when she worked so hard to free him from prison.
He realizes he feels great pain at seeing her captured.

Matthias asks pointed questions of Jarl, learning Yul-Bayur
is imprisoned with the Grisha and Jarl has the master key.
He asks himself when he first knew the *drüskelle*'s mission
was a lie and that the Grisha were not inherently evil. He
hugs his former mentor, then turns the embrace into a
stranglehold that renders Jarl unconscious. He reflects on
his plan to trick Jarl—he's been on Nina's side all along—
takes the key from Jarl and locks him in a cell.

Chapter 36 Summary

Wylan and Jesper hurry to escape the courtyard when six
guards enter, but the guards aren't focused on the Dregs.
Tidemaker Grisha literally "walk through the wall" and
drain the guards' blood until they're dead (387). The
Tidemakers turn on Wylan and Jesper, and Wylan tells

Jesper to use his Fabrikator powers. Jesper focuses on the shards of metal left on his clothes after shaving the gate link and makes them lift and shoot toward the Grisha. The bits of metal burrow all the way to the Grisha's organs, and Jesper wonders if he's "killed two of his kind" as he and Wylan climb to the roof (388).

Chapter 37 Summary

When Matthias returns to Nina's cell and opens the door, Nina realizes he's on her side; "done with fear" (388), they share a passionate embrace. They run to find Yul-Bayur in his prison, which turns out to be an elaborate laboratory containing only a small Shu boy. The boy reveals that his father, Yul-Bayur, died when the Kerch attempted a rescue. They're keeping the boy alive in hopes he can re-create the formula, but the boy is stalling.

Nina asks if he can truly replicate the formula, and the boy thinks he can. Remembering the Grisha tortured by *jurda parem* and her bargain with Matthias, Nina prepares to kill the boy, even though the act would be murder and a betrayal of the Dregs. Matthias protests that the boy is "one of us" (392), and Nina asks for the boy's name, which is Kuwei Yul-Bo. Kuwei makes a flame fly from a beaker, showing he's an Inferni Grisha. His father, also a Grisha, invented *jurda parem* by mistake while trying to hide his son's powers.

Kuwei sets up an explosion with the lab equipment, and the three rush out of the building. The lab explodes, but *drüskelle* capture the three and tie their arms to their sides, leaving the Grisha unable to use their power. One guard, Lars, knows Matthias from their time training together. He taunts the group with a whip attached to their chains and forces them forward. Then blood gushes from Lars's mouth and he drops the whip; a hooded *drüskelle* near him grabs it. The giant ash tree, sacred to the *drüskelle*, begins to fall, and the hooded guard unveils himself: it's Kaz. Kaz nabs Kuwei and, warning the others not to take the *baleen* until they hit bottom, he jumps into the gaping hole beneath the uprooted ash tree—a hole the *drüskelle* believe to be "the throat of Djel" (397), their god. Nina and Matthias, still connected to Kaz by the whip and chains, are pulled into the hole as well.

Chapter 38 Summary

Kaz remembers, earlier that evening, regurgitating the packets of Wylan's root bomb powder he swallowed before entering the prison. He waited for Nina and Matthias and then, when "everything went to hell" (399), he improvised their escape. Kaz pushes *baleen* into Kuwei's mouth and unbinds the others before they fall into the icy water deep beneath the tree. Kaz now knows his suspicions were right: The Ice Court must have been built not around the ash tree, but around the spring beneath, the water source that would explain the Court's moat and deep gorge. Kaz hopes this underground river will deposit them in that gorge before the *baleen* stops working, twelve minutes at most.

As he falls, Kaz remembers, at the age of 14, robbing the bank that helped trick Jordie out of his money. Kaz broke a leg jumping from the bank roof, and "he'd limped ever after" (401). His cane was not a declaration that "no part of him was not broken," but that "no part of him [...] was not stronger for having been broken" (401). Kaz remembers Inej, the way she made him feel "there was magic in this world" (402). Running out of air, he tries to hold onto his desire for revenge, but instead he thinks of Inej—he must live to see her safe.

Chapter 39 Summary

The guards drag Inej back into the palace, near the giant glass enclosure on the second floor. She attacks just as two more guards head toward them, but the two new arrivals turn out to be Jesper and Wylan in disguise. Inej shows them Heleen's diamond choker, which she's stolen because Kaz said they needed a diamond. Wylan attempts to construct a drill from the gate screw and winch, then attaches the diamond to its end. Diamond is the only substance harder than the enclosure's Fabrikator-made glass, and they use the drill to carve a circular opening.

Inej makes a "mad leap" through the hole and grabs the lantern in the enclosure's ceiling. She lands on a large tank and works to control the giant guns attached to it. She successfully shoots one of the guns, making the glass wall "shatter [...] into thousands of glittering pieces" (412). When the smoke clears, Jesper and Wylan descend ropes from the walkway above to meet her. Jesper gets in the driver's seat of the tank, while Inej and Wylan man the guns.

Jesper launches the tank forward, and all three feel the exhilaration of "going out like an army" (413). The tank crashes into the "legendary, impenetrable wall" of the Ice Court (413). They break through and beyond the court, driving down the road.

Chapter 40 Summary

Nina emerges from the water and hears the Ice Court bells in the distance. Matthias pulls Kaz's unconscious body from the river, and Nina uses her Grisha powers to bring back his breath and heartbeat. Nina, Kaz, Matthias and Kuwei run for the harbor and spy the tank that Jesper is driving. Nina spots another column of tanks coming from the Ice Court, and Jesper shoots the bridge over the Ice Court until it collapses, leaving the enemy tanks on the other side.

The entire group climbs onto Jesper's tank, and they drive through towns, past astonished onlookers to the harbor. They arrive at the quay to find over 200 soldiers, "every barrel of every gun [...] pointed directly" at the Dregs (420). A voice demands the release of Kuwei Yul-Bo.

Nina speaks to Kuwei, and he hands her a packet of *jurda parem*, which she ingests. As the drug takes effect, Nina becomes powerful enough to sense the soldiers' bodies as "a map of cells, a thousand equations [...] and she knew only answers" (423).

Chapter 41 Summary

Matthias looks on as Nina, "her skin [...] lit from within" (424), commands the soldiers to sleep. The Dregs walk through the prone soldiers toward the harbor, when another group calls from the quay: Jarl Brum and his *drüskelle* followers. Nina tries to control them, but they wear clothing "reinforced with Grisha steel" (425), so her powers don't affect them. Jarl shoots Matthias in the chest, but the bullet passes through him without leaving a wound; Nina has healed him, and as the *drüskelle* shoot her, she heals herself as well.

Nina forces the soldiers to stand and strip the *drüskelle*, and then she attacks, making them feel terrible pain. Matthias urges Nina to show mercy, and she allows all their attackers to fall back into sleep. They will all survive.

Chapter 42 Summary

Aboard the ship, Nina waits for the drug to wear off, as the entire crew hopes her body can purge the drug without succumbing to addiction. Inej attempts to comfort Nina, and Nina heals the scar left behind from Inej's Menagerie tattoo. Kaz arrives, and Nina leaves him and Inej alone. Inej shares her dream to procure a ship and crew and hunt slavers, but first, she'll return to Ravka to find her family.

Inej wonders what Kaz will do next, what he'll need, and after a long hesitation he asks her to stay in Ketterdam with him. Inej says she'll "have you without armor, Kaz Brekker. Or I will not have you at all" (434). When Kaz doesn't answer, she walks away.

Chapter 43 Summary

Withdrawal symptoms consume Nina: "Her skin [feels] like an enemy" (435). She clings to Matthias, even though touching him hurts, and asks him not to give her more *jurda parem*, no matter how bad her condition gets. He begs for Nina, his "little red bird" (436), not to let go.

Chapter 44 Summary

Wylan uses his knowledge of chemistry to care for Nina, and Jesper "misse[s] having the merchling around to annoy" (437). Jesper also struggles with his own guilt—he wonders if he should have taken *jurda parem* as well, so he could attempt to pull the drug out of Nina's body—but he knows he doesn't have "the makings of a hero" (438). The boat lands in Ketterdam, and Jesper accompanies Kaz in a longboat to Fifth Harbor, where they'll meet the Merchant Council. Jesper still wonders what he'll do now—does "he want to cultivate his [Grisha] power or keep hiding it?" (439).

Kaz delivers a note to the Council, explaining the truth of the mission. The next morning at dawn, Jesper, Kaz, Matthias, Inej, and Kuwei head out to meet the Council representative on Vellgeluk, an isolated island. Wylan has stayed behind to care for Nina, and Jesper hopes the boy isn't avoiding him.

The elder Van Eck, a Shu representative, and guards, some carrying a heavy trunk, come to meet the Dregs. Kaz opens the trunk, and Jesper sees "row after row" (443) of Kerch bills inside. Kaz ensures all the money is there and the crew prepares to leave—but Van Eck responds, "[T]here's no way any of you are getting off this island" (443). Suddenly a "howling, unnatural gale" rises (444): The sailors of Van Eck's ship are Squallers, dosed with *jurda parem*.

Chapter 45 Summary

Kaz points out that if the Merchant Council reneges on their deal, no one from the Barrel will work with them, but Van Eck reveals the Council was never involved. Kaz has been duped— "Hertzoon and his coffeehouse all over again" (445)—as Van Eck wanted the power of *jurda parem* for himself. He's already buying *jurda* fields, and when the chaos of *jurda parem* overtakes the world, he plans to be its master.

Van Eck orders the Grisha to smash the small longboat with a wave, and then the Grisha send a much larger wave toward the *Ferolind*. Kaz reveals that Wylan is on the ship, but Van Eck doesn't care; although Wylan is a genius with equations, he can't read or write. Van Eck cast Wylan out as a disgrace, and the letters he sent Wylan were only to mock him.

Jesper defends Wylan, saying he's "smarter than most of us put together, and he deserves a better father" (448), before two giant waves crush the *Ferolind*. The boy whom Van Eck believes to be Kuwei speaks in "perfect, unaccented Kerch" (449); it's Wylan, tailored by Nina to look like Kuwei. Wylan himself came up with the plan as a way to test his father's true feelings.

Kaz demands that Van Eck let them free with their payment—only then will he reveal the true Kuwei's location. Van Eck orders his guards to kill everyone except Kaz, and Kaz instinctively looks to Inej, the girl he cares for, which prompts Van Eck to demand his guards capture Inej. A fight ensues, and one of the Grisha scoops up Inej and flies into the sky. Van Eck gives Kaz a week to deliver Kuwei "or they'll hear that girl's screams all the way back in Fjerda" (452). Although Jesper has a clear shot at Van Eck, Kaz tells him to let the mercher go.

Once Van Eck and his crew are gone, Kaz thinks of Nina and Kuwei safe in the cages at Hellsgate, which have been empty since Matthias's prison break. Jesper berates Wylan for taking such a risk, and then Kaz accuses Jesper of having "sold us out to Pekka Rollins" (453). Jesper had told a Dime Lion he would be getting "big money" soon, trying to buy more time to repay his debts. Jesper tries to defend himself, but Kaz wants to fight; only Matthias's intervention keeps them apart.

Wylan speaks up for Jesper, saying he made a mistake but didn't intend to betray anyone. They wait for the *Ferolind's* captain to pick them up, and Kaz determines that while he's made mistakes of his own, he won't "let himself be bested by some thieving merch" (455). The rest of the crew recognizes Kaz's "scheming face," and Kaz asks for the others' help to get Inej back. They all agree, and Kaz is "Dirtyhands" once more, "come to see the rough work done" (456).

Chapter 46 Summary

In his office above the Emerald Palace, Pekka studies the crew before him: Kaz, Nina with "jutting bones" and "trembling hands" (457), and the rest of Kaz's crew. Pekka recalls that Kaz had let Pekka go back in the Ice Court, telling Pekka "you weren't meant to die here" (459). Now, Kaz has "come to collect" (459): He needs 2,000 *kruge* from Pekka to help him wage war against Van Eck. In return, Kaz will sell his shares in the Crow Club and Fifth Harbor. Pekka agrees to the deal, recognizing a darkness in Kaz that sends "a chill slithering up his spine" (461).

Kaz and his crew leave, and Pekka realizes Kaz has stolen his watch, his wallet and even his gold shoe buckles. Pekka hopes Van Eck will kill Kaz—because if he doesn't, Pekka will have to kill Kaz himself.

Chapters 35-46 Analysis

Matthias finally realizes that Nina, like all of the Grisha, is not a monster, and he rejects the *drüskelle* for a new family consisting of Nina and the rest of the Dregs. Matthias takes his long-awaited revenge on Nina by locking her behind bars, but he feels only pain rather than satisfaction. A life of hatred and revenge, Matthias has learned, is a "poison [he] can drink […] no longer" (385). Matthias now understands monsters are defined by their behavior rather than by their magical powers. Grisha like other humans, have "potential to do great good, and also great harm"

(383). Treating Grisha as tools to be used, experimented on and destroyed, would "make Matthias the monster" that Brum had become (383).

Nina displays her very human nature shortly after Matthias breaks her out of her cell, when she has the chance to kill a young teen and prevent the formula for *jurda parem* from being unleashed. Matthias tells Nina the boy, Kuwei, is "one of us"— "a boy not much younger than she was, caught up in a war he hadn't chosen for himself" (392). Nina realizes she can't kill the innocent teen, to whom she feels a connection, and Kuwei finds an instant home among the Dregs. Like them, he is a survivor in a cruel world that ripped away his home and family.

While Matthias and Nina rescue Kuwei, Kaz nearly drowns during a risky escape through an underground spring. His thoughts while at death's door reveal that love is more powerful than vengeance. Desperate to survive, Kaz "trie[s] to think of his brother, of revenge" (403), but the only thing that motivates him is his need to tell Inej "that she was lovely and brave and better than anything he deserved" (403). For Inej, Kaz is willing to "pull himself together into some semblance of a man" (403), to embrace his better self rather than his vindictive criminal nature. Human connection proves stronger than the desire for revenge, bringing out the nobility in the characters.

While the Dregs work together to pull off the ultimate "magic trick" of escaping from the Ice Court, they face a final challenge that requires them to use *jurda parem*, the dangerous drug that has loomed over the entire novel. When the crew faces down a huge army, Nina sacrifices herself by taking *jurda parem*. Her choice again shows she is human rather than monster, willing to risk dying from withdrawal to save her friends, and her transformation under the influence of the drug emphasizes the formidable threat the drug represents. Nina becomes powerful enough to command an entire army, and Matthias tells her the *drüskelle* now "fear you as I once feared you" and "as you once feared me"—for "we are all someone's monster" (427). In an act of humanity rather than monstrosity, Nina allows her enemies—including Brum—to fall into sleep rather than death.

On the ship back to Ketterdam, Nina fights through withdrawal with Matthias by her side, the two now bound together by love. The other characters also wrestle with the changes they've undergone throughout their quest. Inej tells Kaz about her plan to hunt down slavers, and she offers Kaz one more chance to convince her to stay with him. When Kaz doesn't respond, it becomes clear he can't make himself completely vulnerable and let go of the Dirtyhands persona he's constructed. Inej walks away, choosing her own purpose over her love for Kaz.

Jesper misses spending time with Wylan, who is tending to Nina, while he simultaneously wrestles with guilt over not volunteering to take *jurda parem*. He questions how he will deal with the now exposed secret of his Grisha heritage; he doesn't come to a satisfactory answer by the end of the novel, but he does finally discover the truth behind Wylan's past and stands up for the boy he loves. Wylan cannot return home, but he has found another one. He belongs among the teenagers of the Dregs, all of whom have lost their own home in one way or another.

Bardugo ends her novel where she began it, by emphasizing that the respectable world of merchants and the criminal underworld are not so different. The mercher Van Eck is, if anything, less concerned with morals and empathy than the Dregs. He is willing to unleash the chaos of *jurda parem* on the world, causing great suffering as long as he can be chaos's wealthy master. The ending also cements Bardugo's Ketterdam as a land of treachery and deceit, where Kaz and his team—the ultimate tricksters—have now been conned themselves.

While *Six of Crow*'s central character, Kaz, has resolved to become a better version of himself to win Inej's love, the novel ends with the assertion that in an immoral world, that the better person always ends up dead. To save Inej after Van Eck kidnaps her, Kaz must again embrace the worst part of himself. He once again seeks revenge and enlisting the rest of the Dregs to help him. This time, however, the Dregs work together as a family, determined to save one of their own; it's a noble mission, even if they'll take any unscrupulous measures necessary to accomplish it.

Kaz Brekker

Seventeen-year-old Kaz Brekker, second-in-command of the Dregs gang, is known as Dirtyhands because of the unscrupulous methods he employs. While elderly Per Haskell is the Dregs' official leader, Kaz has made himself, as one opposing gang member puts it, "the spine of Haskell's operation" (25). In the five years since he joined the Dregs, Kaz has transformed the gang from a laughingstock to a power player in the Barrel, Ketterdam's criminal district. He's established the successful Crow Club gambling hall and made the Barrel's Fifth Harbor into a thriving spot for the Dregs to pick up marks. Following a lifelong fascination with magic tricks, Kaz has become adept at both physical illusions and mental trickery. He uses "information"—the shameful secrets he learns about his victims—to maintain his upper hand.

Kaz dresses in elegant tailored clothes, seeing no difference between a businessman and a thief. He makes no secret of his lack of morals, claiming to act purely out of greed and content to be known as a monster. Even Kaz's apparent weakness becomes a part of his invulnerable image: Although Kaz has limped since breaking his leg in a fall at age 14, he carries an elegant cane carved with a crow's head and makes the cane "part of the myth he built" (401). Though he has been broken, he is "stronger for having been broken," and proudly calls himself "bastard of the Barrel" (401). Along with the cane, Kaz wears gloves at all times, and offers no reason for doing so—an element of mystery that only adds to the legend of "Dirtyhands."

Kaz can orchestrate complex takedowns, as he does when he lays a trap for a rival gang. He can also act with brutality if necessary; for example, when he yanks out an enemy's eyeball to force him to talk. Throughout the novel, Kaz's desire for vengeance forces him to confront his own vulnerability and question his mission of revenge. When Kaz enters the White Court as a prisoner, he is stripped of his cane and more importantly, his gloves, and has to contend with his phobia of physical touch. Only Inej's comforting presence brings him "back to some semblance of sanity" (281), but he can't let go of his mental armor. When he doesn't express his love for Inej, she rejects his offer; when she is kidnapped, Kaz again shuts down his emotions and becomes the ruthless bastard of the Barrel once more.

Inej Ghafa

Sixteen-year-old Inej Ghafa, known as "the Wraith" among the Dregs, grew up among the Suli people, a nomadic tribe in Ravka. As part of a family of acrobats, Inej learned to balance on the high-wire and aerial swings; as Kaz's closest ally in the Dregs, she uses her agility to spy and attack when least expected. Inej is so adept Kaz thinks "cats would sit attentively at her feet to learn her methods" (38), and she's ruthless with her knives when she or her friends are in danger.

Over the course of *Six of Crows*, Inej's past is gradually revealed: At age fourteen she was kidnapped by slavers on the coast of Ravka, taken to Ketterdam and sold to Heleen Van Houden, proprietor of the Menagerie, a brothel specializing in "exotics." Heleen beat Inej, "bought her once, and then sold her again and again" (367), and Inej struggles with both fury and fear of Heleen throughout the novel. Inej first encountered Kaz at the Menagerie—he paid Heleen for information—and told him she could be a useful asset to the Dregs, so Kaz convinced the Dregs' leader to purchase Inej's indenture. Inej believes that Kaz has "turned her into a spy" (63), he's given her the ability to stand up for herself. She can't help but care for Kaz even when he doesn't "seem to give a second thought to her presence" (66).

At the beginning of the novel, Inej is motivated by what she *doesn't* want. Desperate to be free of all remnants of the Menagerie, she exchanged her Menagerie tattoo for a vicious scar, yet she won't take the Dregs tattoo, either. As the story continues, Inej discovers where to "aim" her own heart: She dreams of commanding her own ship and "hunt[ing] the slavers and their buyers" (311). Inej still cares for Kaz, and although he asks her to stay with him, he can't speak his true feelings for Inej. She chooses her own quest to vanquish the slavers over her attachment to Kaz, but as the novel ends, Inej is kidnapped, and her fate is left to be decided in the novel's sequel.

Nina Zenik

Nina Zenik is a 17-year-old Grisha Heartrender, meaning she has the ability to magically influence the human body "to kill or to cure" (76). She is also outspoken, confident, and skilled at talking herself out of difficult situations—in multiple languages—as well as using her Grisha powers. Originally from Ravka, Nina joined the Grisha's Second Army after Ravka's civil war, eager to fight for the people and country she loved. She was captured by Fjerdan Grisha hunters and only escaped when the Fjerdans' ship sunk. She managed to reach Kerch on a merchant ship, but along the way she developed a complex relationship with one of the *drüskelle*, Matthias Helvar.

For the first portion of *Six of Crows*, Nina's actions are governed alternately by her desire to make up for betraying

Matthias and her loyalty to the Grisha. Nina wants to keep the formula for *jurda parem* secret—the drug will destroy the Grisha if it's placed in the wrong hands—and she's willing to kill its inventor to do so. Nina is torn between her love for Matthias and her hatred for the way Matthias and his countrymen see Grisha as an abomination. When Matthias betrays his own mentors to save Nina, Nina fully accepts her feelings for Matthias, promising to "kiss [him] unconscious" (390). Then, when she has the chance to kill Yul-Bayur's son Kuwei, betray the Dregs, and ensure the Grisha's safety, she chooses not to. She has now placed her own personal relationships, and her sense of human decency, above killing in the Grisha's name.

In the climax of the novel, Nina takes her new loyalty to her friends even further, displaying great courage as she takes *jurda parem*—a drug that could leave her an addict, withering away till she dies—so she'll have the power to save the Dregs. She does save her friends, but as the novel ends, she is still weak from withdrawal, with another character guessing "she might not last out the month" (457). She professes her love for Matthias and her desire to return home to Ravka. Her two conflicting desires have now come together as Matthias promises to take her there. Most of all, Nina feels no regret for her choice to sacrifice herself, placing her friends' and love's lives above her own.

Matthias Helvar

Eighteen-year-old Matthias Helvar is from Fjerda, where he was a *drüskelle,* a hunter of Grisha on an intensely personal mission. Matthias's parents and sisters were killed when Grisha soldiers burned his village, and *drüskelle* leader Jarl Brum became his father and mentor. Matthias believes that Grisha are abominations; he is faithful to the nature gods of his country and, as Grisha's powers are "unnatural," they must be exterminated. At the same time, Matthias can't deny his deep attraction to Nina, the Grisha who saved him from drowning in the shipwreck and then falsely accused him, so he ended up in prison.

Kaz, whom Matthias despises for his ruthless nature, asks Matthias to help him break into the Ice Court, an act that will force Matthias to "betray his country" (111). The only way Kaz can convince Matthias is by offering him an official pardon from Nina's false charges, a way for Matthias to become a *drüskelle* again. The desire to return to the position that means so much to him—and, once he does so, to make Nina pay—convinces Matthias to betray his country by guiding outsiders into the sacred court. Matthias considers compromising his morals out of a desire for revenge.

As Matthias comes to know and care for the rest of the Dregs—and, despite himself, allows his love for Nina to overtake his hatred—his motivations transform. He decides to truly help the Dregs, even imprisoning his former mentor, Jarl Brum. After Nina sacrifices herself by taking *jurda parem*, Matthias stays beside her through her withdrawal, promising to take her back to Ravka and begging her not to go. In the final scene of the novel, Matthias protects a still-weak Nina as the Dregs begin their next mission. Clearly, his love for her has become his new purpose, his honor and driving force.

Jesper Fahey

The son of a farmer in Novyi Zem, 17-year-old Jesper Fahey traveled to Ketterdam to attend university but ended up joining the Dregs. Inej describes Jesper as a long-limbed sharpshooter who is "constantly in motion" (17); only Jesper himself knows that the thrill of a gunfight serves a deeper purpose, "call[ing] the scattered, irascible, permanently seeking part of his mind into focus" (142). This same "seeking" aspect of his personality originally drew Jesper to Ketterdam, where he hoped studying would satisfy his restlessness, but he found that gambling did so even better. Jesper loves and misses his father, but he can't handle the countryside's "wide open spaces and silence" (192), and he feels incredible guilt for borrowing his father's money and losing it while gambling. Jesper joins Kaz's dangerous mission because his portion of the reward will allow him to pay back his father, and he maintains this motivation throughout the novel.

Despite his gambling problem, Jesper demonstrates great bravery and loyalty to his friends. He works particularly hard to protect Wylan, a mercher's son and the least experienced of the crew. Although Jesper taunts Wylan, the jabs become increasingly playful until Jesper concedes that "flirting with [Wylan] might actually be more fun than annoying him" (291). Jesper eventually admits to liking boys in addition to girls, and Jesper's and Wylan's relationship seems set to develop further in the novel's sequel.

At the same time, Jesper's role in the Dregs' mission forces him to expose a part of his identity he's always concealed: He is a Grisha Fabrikator, able to control materials such as metal, and he has kept his powers hidden at his father's urging. He realizes that once the mission is complete, he'll have to decide whether to "cultivate his power or keep hiding it" (439)—a decision he still hasn't made when the novel ends. Jesper clearly has some work left to do in order to manage his impulsive nature, understand his Grisha abilities, and move forward in his romantic relationship with Wylan.

Wylan Van Eck

Wylan, the 16-year-old son of mercher Jan Van Eck, becomes part of Kaz's mission both because he understands explosives and because, as the son of the man promising their reward, Wylan is the Dregs' "guarantee on 30 million *kruge*" (119). Wylan ran away from his father's home three months before Kaz's mission began, and the reason remains a secret until the very end of the novel, when Van Eck himself reveals it. Although Wylan is a talented musician and scientist, he can't read, and Van Eck considers his son "a moron" and "a disgrace to my house" (447). Van Eck has no qualms about letting Wylan die along with the other Dregs. Wylan must search for acceptance and community outside of his biological family.

For much of the book, Wylan is often "red-faced and mortified" (119), dealing with both the unfamiliar violence and coarseness around him, and the taunts of the other Dregs. At the same time, he stands up for himself, insisting "I'm not useless" (121), and doing all he can to prove his words true. Even before the Dregs leave Ketterdam, Wylan begins to prove his worth by setting off bombs that allow the crew to escape an ambush. Wylan looks for community among the Dregs, even though as a rich merchant's son, he is out of his element with these experienced criminals.

As the mission continues, Wylan grows increasingly close with Jesper in particular—Jesper is tasked with watching out for the boy, and they're often paired for assignments. Wylan finds the courage to ask Jesper if he only likes girls, and Jesper admits that he does not. Now secure that he helped the Dregs complete their mission, and that he has Jesper's respect—and possibly something more—Wylan stands up to his father at the end of the novel.

The Search for Home

The six main characters of *Six of Crows* are all outcasts
who have either chosen to leave or been forced out of their
childhood homes. Coming from disparate backgrounds,
these characters are united by the fact they've had to fend
for themselves, to survive on their own as teenagers in a
cruel adult world. Throughout the novel, the protagonists
struggle in different ways to either find a way to return
home—or accept the fact they can never do so. In the end,
they must redefine the concept of "home" altogether.

Kaz Brekker, the central character who brings together this
crew of misfits, claims to have no home or family, proudly
calling himself the "the bastard of the Barrel" (303). As the
novel continues, readers learn that Kaz *did* have a home in
Kerch, until his father and older brother both died, leaving
Kaz alone in the dangerous Barrel district. Of all the
characters, Kaz is perhaps most vehement in his rejection
of the concept of home: He takes on a fake last name to
hide any traces of his old identity and rids himself of all
traces of empathy, transforming himself into the "monster"
Dirtyhands. Even as Dirtyhands, Kaz holds onto his love
for his brother and hopes to punish those who caused his
brother's death. Though he might not want to admit it, Kaz
does understand the importance of home and family, and he
uses that knowledge to motivate the rest of his crew.

Kaz specifically uses the concept of home to entice
Matthias, a Fjerdan guided by "honor" to join a gang of
criminals he would otherwise avoid. Kaz promises Matthias
a pardon that will allow him to return to his *drüskelle*
community in Fjerda, and Matthias wants to return to his
home so badly that "the longing for it twisted in his chest"

(115). Nina, a Grisha from Ravka, also desperately wants to go back to her home and her people, with a desire so great it's "a physical ache" (299). When Matthias does return to his homeland during the Dregs' mission, he finds that coming home is not so simple as he expected: The Ice Court seems to be "home turned on its head, his life viewed at the wrong angle" (343). Similarly, Nina realizes that her desire to be with Matthias is as great as her loyalty to the Ravkan Grisha. At the end of the novel, Matthias suggests that if Nina wants to return to Ravka, they should do so together.

Like Matthias and Nina, Inej lost her homeland through an act of violence, when she was kidnapped by slavers and sold to a brothel in Ketterdam. While Inej lived in Ravka, her Suli family were nomads for whom "'home' really just meant family" (265). Inej longs to see her family again, but at the same time she can't "bear the thought of returning," as she doubts she'll be "forgiven" for the person she's become since being sold to a pleasure house. Because of the violence, greed, and hatred in her world, Inej, like Nina and Matthias, must find a new sense of home and purpose. She conceives of a different life for herself, one in which she hunts down slavers and seeks vengeance for others who have been taken from their families and homes.

Unlike Nina, Matthias, and Inej, the two remaining members of Kaz's crew chose to leave homes where they didn't belong. Jesper wasn't satisfied by the "wide open spaces and silence" of his country home (192), and he moved to Ketterdam hoping a university education would stimulate his restless mind, but he found that gambling did so even more. Wylan driven out of a wealthy home by a father who couldn't accept the fact that his son couldn't read. He searches for a new home among the Dregs and finds one through the others' respect and acceptance—and through a budding romance with Jesper.

By the end of *Six of Crows*, the members of Kaz's mission find their status as outcasts has actually "bound them together" (332)—they are united by their loss of family, by the fact that "if one or all of them disappeared tonight, on one would come looking" (332). Ultimately, the characters' ability to survive the loss of home, and the loss of the security home and family provides, has drawn them together despite their vastly different backgrounds. Home can be found in shared experience and purpose as much as it can be found in a place or a biological relationship.

Vengeance

Kaz's overwhelming desire to seek revenge for his brother's death sets the novel's entire plot into motion. The thirst for vengeance can drive a person away from their true nature, destroying both of themselves and others around them. For characters like Kaz and Matthias, redemption comes not through revenge but through stronger relationships with the people for whom they care. At the same time, a different sort of vengeance can become a noble purpose, as it does for Inej by the end of the novel.

Kaz's criminal persona, Dirtyhands, grows out of his anger at those who have wronged him and his brother. In order to exact vengeance—to make those who wronged him and his brother pay—Kaz transforms himself into a monster willing to harm innocents and act solely in self-interest. He has no qualms about recruiting five other teenagers, including Inej, the girl for whom he cares most, for what is likely a suicide mission—so long as that mission takes down his worst enemy. Another member of the crew Kaz recruits for this suicide mission, Matthias, is also motivated by vengeance in a way that brings out his worst aspects. Matthias aligns with a "demon's crew," giving up the sacred secrets of his homeland for the chance to "run Nina Zenik to ground and make her pay in every way imaginable" (116).

As Kaz and Matthias grow closer to Inej and Nina, respectively, they find that feelings of love and loyalty begin to trump the desire for revenge. When Inej nearly dies fending off an ambush meant to sabotage the mission, Kaz tries to remind himself of his goals: "Money. Vengeance. Jordie's voice in my head silenced forever" (205). As the mission continues, Kaz finds that instead of revenge, "all he [can] think of [is] Inej" (403). Unlike the desire for vengeance, which leaves Kaz willing to sacrifice both friends and enemies, love for Inej makes Kaz want to better himself, to "pull himself together into some semblance of a man for her" (403).

Mattias finds that the more he spends time with Nina, the more he questions his desire for revenge. At one point, Matthias must pretend to imprison Nina, to trick an enemy into believing they're on the same side. He is acting out a scene he'd dreamed of— "he had longed to see her made captive, punished as he had been punished" (381)—yet he finds the act only brings him pain. Matthias realizes that seeking revenge would make him a monster, so he forgives Nina and lets his love for her drive his actions in the remainder of the novel.

What Makes a Monster

Near the end of *Six of Crows*, Matthias tells Nina, "We are all someone's monster" (427). Throughout the novel, characters become monstrous, either willingly, as Kaz does, or because others see them as terribly inhuman. Only an acknowledgment of shared humanity can reveal the person beneath the monstrous mask.

Monstrosity appears early on in the novel, when Inej thinks that Kaz has become the "monster" Dirtyhands in order "to see the rough work done" (32). Kaz embraces his monstrous reputation, telling Inej, "When everyone knows you're a monster, you needn't waste time doing every monstrous thing" (38), and he welcomes the rumors that he has "claws and not fingers" (58) underneath his ever-present gloves. Matthias refers to Kaz as "*demjin*," or demon, throughout the book, underscoring Kaz's perceived inhumanity. By the end of the novel, Kaz must choose whether to embrace his human or monstrous side. Although love for Inej has brought out his humanity, as Kaz hopes to become "some semblance of a man" for Inej (403), he must once again don his Dirtyhands persona to rescue her after she is kidnapped.

Although Kaz may have earned the title of *demjin* through his actions, other characters inherited their identity as monsters. Nina remarks that over countless years, "Grisha had come to be viewed as monsters by the Fjerdans" (357); Nina, a Grisha with magical powers, becomes a "witch" an "abomination," but most of all, a "monster" in the eyes of the Fjerdan Matthias. Nina sees the Fjerdan *drüskelle* like Matthias, who hunt and execute Grisha, as cruel, monstrous hunters. Nina's attitude is exemplified by her characterization of the *drüskelle*'s leader Jarl Brum, whom she describes as a "monster waiting in the dark" (168). Matthias reveals to Nina that Grisha slaughtered his family during a raid, and Nina comes to understand how Grisha could be monstrous in his eyes. Yet she finds it equally disturbing to learn Matthias "think[s] of that monster Brum as some kind of father figure" (236), since Brum took Matthias in after the massacre.

The definition of "monster" shifts based on who is doing the defining; by the end of the novel, the characters actively resist viewing each other as monsters, seeing each other's humanity instead. While the Grisha may have inhuman, demonic-seeming powers, they are humans "like anyone else—full of the potential to do great good, and also great harm" (383). Monstrosity is defined less by one's nature and more by one's actions.

Jurda Parem

Jurda parem, a drug that gives Grisha the power to control others' minds, to walk through walls, and to transform lead into gold, drives the plot of *Six of Crows* as well as illustrating the dangers of absolute power and greed. The mercher Jan Van Eck explains that *jurda parem* "seems to sharpen and hone a Grisha's senses," so that "things become possible that simply shouldn't be" (48). A Grisha under the influence of *jurda parem* can compel a man to chop off his own finger; the drug becomes an ominous, inhuman element that inspires fear and dread. Anyone who controls *parem* can control the world. Although Kaz and his crew agree to retrieve the scientist with the formula for *parem* for their personal gain, they also understand that the fate of the world hangs in the balance.

The symbol of *jurda parem* becomes even more formidable as "the drug clearly came with a price" (48), and a high one: The drug can cause addiction with only one dose, making it almost inconceivably powerful, and withdrawal symptoms usually lead to death. This contradiction—a Grisha made inhumanly strong by the drug then left desperately weak without it—adds complexity to the drug as a symbol of power. When Nina takes *parem* to save herself and her friends, she appears as if a "god's power flowed through her" (424), and she is able to command an entire army. Once the drug wears off, she becomes too weak to stand, in so much pain that "her skin felt like an enemy" (435).

The drug's other association—greed—becomes clear when the Dregs learn that Van Eck wanted the power of *jurda parem* for himself. Van Eck has been buying all the *jurda* fields he can; once he has the formula for *parem,* he will be the world's "very wealthy master" (446). Van Eck knows he can capitalize on the rest of the world's desire for power— "every government will be clamoring" for *parem* (446)—to feed his own greed. He doesn't care about the lives of the Grisha, of Kaz and his friends, and of the many others who might be destroyed in the process. Although *jurda parem* is a destructive drug, in the end it is only a tool. True destruction comes from the greed, power, and ruthlessness *parem* enables—qualities that are wielded by humans.

Magic Tricks and Sleight of Hand

Kaz's fascination with magic tricks led to his brother Jordie's downfall; young Kaz convinced Jordie to take him to see a magician near the gambling hall where his brother fell for a cruel scam. Just as Kaz chose to conquer the brutal, crime-ridden Barrel that destroyed his family, he also masters magicians' trickery and uses his skill to craft a more powerful image.

Before his brother's death, Kaz was already obsessed with sleight of hand: The mystery of how a magician made a coin disappear "kept him up at night" (207). After Jordie's demise, Kaz goes much further, realizing "a good magician wasn't much different from a proper thief" (315), using sleight of hand to steal, cheat while gambling, and take others by surprise. Kaz's skill contributes to his formidable reputation in the Barrel, and he graduates to a more advanced form of magic trick, one involving the mind. He trades in information, stealing intel and using it to take down his enemies. He also gathers others skilled at trickery to his cause, such as Inej, whose acrobatic skill allows her to move so silently she can "simply erase herself" (40).

The Dregs' quest throughout the novel—to break a prisoner out of the most secure fortress in the world—is itself a magic trick, and Kaz uses mental trickery to devise a plan. Inej also uses her skill in almost superhuman ways, climbing up a hot incinerator shaft, while Jesper employs his sharp-shooting skills, Wylan his genius with bomb-making, and Jesper and Nina their Grisha magic. Their group magic trick works, but in the end, the Dregs find themselves victims of another trick, as the mercher who sent them on the prison mission double-crosses them and kidnaps Inej. In the final pages of the novel, Matthias observes that Kaz is "digging in [his] bag of tricks" again (455), as he concocts a scheme to get Inej back and take revenge on the merchant.

Pigeons and Crows

Near the opening of *Six of Crows,* Kaz remembers his and his brothers' first days in the big city and "hate[s] the boys they'd been, two stupid pigeons waiting to be plucked" (71). "Pigeon" is the gang members' term for an innocent to be duped and taken advantage of; Jesper tells newbie Wylan about "The *mark*, the pigeon, the cozy, the fool you're looking to fleece" (126). Kaz distances himself from the "pigeon" he once was by taking on the symbolism of a different bird: the dark, wily crow who fends for himself and always comes out on top. Kaz names his business venture the Crow Club, the Dregs' gang tattoo includes an image of a crow, and Kaz's cane has a carved crow on top. The cane, which should represent Kaz's weakness, becomes a symbol of his ability to use wits and trickery to come out on top. Thus, the crow marks his transformation from prey to creature of power.

Taking the novel's bird symbolism further, the author describes the Ice Court prison as "one big white pigeon ready for the plucking" (128)—and Kaz and his co-conspirators successfully pluck that pigeon, using trickery to complete their quest. In one final twist, the merchant who contracted Kaz's services kidnaps Kaz's right hand, Inej, and once again makes Kaz the pigeon rather than the crow. Kaz considers himself "dumber than a pigeon fresh off the boat" to have been duped by Van Eck (453), and he vows to take revenge as the novel ends.

No Mourners, No Funerals

Throughout *Six of Crows*, the Dregs repeat the call-and-response phrase "no mourners, no funerals" as a good-luck recitation before missions. The phrase becomes a motif that indicates a dangerous situation is about to take place, increasing suspense throughout the novel. The meaning of the words—the idea that the gang members won't stop to miss or honor those who die—adds deeper dimension to the repeated phrase, illustrating the cruel world in which these characters live.

While the main characters of the novel are only teenagers, they've already witnessed, been victims to, and perpetrated acts of violence. Many have lost family members and friends to war and crime. To survive, the characters have had to harden themselves, trusting no one and putting their own interests first, so they will have no more losses to mourn. Over the course of the novel, the main characters come to care for each other deeply, to the point where they risk their own safety for one another. When the phrase appears later in the novel, it transforms into a reminder that their group is "bound together." Even Matthias, who considers himself above gang culture, "mutter[s] the words softly" along with the others (332). The motto expresses camaraderie and a deeper connection that brings the novel's

young protagonists together and helps them survive in a
violent world.

IMPORTANT QUOTES

1. "Kaz Brekker didn't need a reason. Those were the words whispered on the streets of Ketterdam, in the taverns and coffeehouses, in the dark and bleeding alleys of the pleasure district known as the Barrel. The boy they called Dirtyhands didn't need a reason any more than he needed permission—to break a leg, sever an alliance, or change a man's fortunes with the turn of a card.

   Of course they were wrong, Inej considered as she crossed the bridge over the black waters of the Beurskanal to the deserted main square that fronted the Exchange. Every act of violence was deliberate, and every favor came with enough strings attached to stage a puppet show. Kaz always had his reasons. Inej could just never be sure they were good ones. Especially tonight." (Chapter 2, Page 15)

   This quote introduces both the novel's central character, 17-year-old gang leader Kaz Brenner, and Kaz's deliberately constructed identity: Dirtyhands. With his ruthless willingness to destroy others, Dirtyhands seems almost inhuman, a mysterious figure skilled at tricking his enemies, and lacking any morals to restrict his actions. The quote also introduces the violent, merciless world the novel's characters inhabit, one that forces a teenager like Kaz to become a hardened criminal.

2. "Most gang members in the Barrel loved flash: gaudy waistcoats, watch fobs studded with false gems,

trousers in every print and pattern imaginable. Kaz was the exception—the picture of restraint, his dark vests and trousers simply cut and tailored along severe lines. At first, she'd thought it was a matter of taste, but she'd come to understand that it was a joke he played on the upstanding merchers. He enjoyed looking like one of them.

'I'm a businessman,' he'd told her. 'No more, no less.'

'You're a thief, Kaz.'

'Isn't that what I just said?'" (Chapter 2, Page 23)

This quotation continues to establish Kaz's careful creation of his own identity, as he controls his physical appearance to impress his colleagues and enemies. Unlike his competitors', Kaz's clothing says he doesn't need "flash" to proclaim his might. Moreover, Kaz's sartorial choices emphasize the novel's ambiguous morality: In the world Bardugo has created, respectable merchants and criminals are equally motivated by greed and self-interest. Kaz's comparison of merchers and thieves even foreshadows the novel's final twist, in which a prominent businessman is willing to betray his word and take lives for his own personal gain.

3. "Geels looked at Kaz as if he was finally seeing him for the first time. The boy he'd been talking to had been cocky, reckless, easily amused, but not frightening—not really. Now the monster was here, dead-eyed and unafraid. Kaz Brenner was gone, and Dirtyhands had come to see the rough work done." (Chapter 2, Page 32)

*The author introduces the novel's theme of "monsters,"
contrasting the human character of Kaz with the
"monster" Dirtyhands, a constructed, inhuman persona
who lacks empathy and fear. Kaz has just told his
opponent Geels that he's prepared to murder Geels's
sweetheart if Geels doesn't give in to his demands. As
the quote illustrates, surviving in a cruel world like the
Barrel requires Kaz to become cruel himself, to the
point where he would murder an innocent to
accomplish his goals.*

4. "Kaz laughed. 'What's the difference between
   wagering at the Crow Club and speculating on the floor
   of the Exchange?'
   'One is theft and the other is commerce.'
   'When a man loses his money, he may have trouble
   telling them apart.'" (Chapter 3, Page 43)

   *This quote illustrates the immoral nature of the society
   Bardugo has created, where merchants and criminals
   alike try to trick others out of their livelihood. Bardugo
   tells the story through the point of view of criminals—
   antiheroes who don't automatically elicit the reader's
   sympathy—but at the same time she emphasizes that the
   supposedly "respectable" members of society act in
   equally reprehensible ways. The quote also
   foreshadows the betrayals yet to be revealed in the
   novel: When the protagonists trust those who appear to
   be upstanding citizens and people of authority, they find
   themselves taken advantage of as a result.*

5. "Matthias knew monsters, and one glance at Kaz
   Brekker had told him this was a creature who had spent
   too long in the dark—he'd brought something back

with him when he'd crawled into the light." (Chapter 7, Page 110)

Bardugo develops the theme of monsters, and how tragic circumstances can lead a person to become monstrous. Matthias recognizes the way Kaz has abandoned compassion and created a cruel, even heartless persona for himself. At the same time, a character's monstrous nature is defined by the person who views them: Matthias thinks he "knows" monsters such as the Grisha, but as the novel continues, he'll question whether the Grisha really are monsters just because they possess magic. In the same way, Matthias will reassess his view of Kaz, as both he and readers come to see why Kaz has become Dirtyhands.

6. "He would run Nina Zevik to ground and make her pay in every way imaginable. Death would be too good. He'd have her thrown into the most miserable cell in the Ice Court, where she'd never be warm again. He'd toy with her as she'd toyed with him." (Chapter 7, Page 116)

This quote emphasizes the theme of vengeance and the way it can damage those who desire it. Matthias's need to take revenge on Nina consumes him, warping his vision so he can't see the reality of the situation: the fact that Nina actually tried to save him rather than "toying" with him. Matthias characterizes Nina as less than human, as a witch who plays with him and who doesn't deserve compassion. As he spends more time with Nina, his viewpoint begins to change, and he realizes that vengeance may not offer true satisfaction.

7. "*Move,* she told herself. *This is a stupid place to die.* And yet a voice in her head said there were worse places. She would die here, in freedom, beneath the beginnings of dawn. She'd die after a worthy fight, not because some man had tired of her or required more from her than she could give. Better to die here by her own blade than with her face painted and her body swathed in false silks." (Chapter 12, Page 151)

Inej is seriously injured while protecting the other Dregs during an ambush, and she prepares to kill herself rather than be captured. The scene both underscores how dangerous the Dregs' mission will be—they haven't even begun their task, and already one of their strongest members has nearly died—and reveals important aspects of Inej's past and her perspective. Inej is haunted by her time in the Menagerie pleasure house, where she was forced to become an object for men to use, with a "painted" face and "false silks." Now, Inej values free will so much that she places it above her own safety, and even her survival.

8. "In school, Nina had been obsessed with the *drüskelle.* They'd been the creatures of her nightmares with their white wolves and their cruel knives and the horses they bred for battle with Grisha. It was why she'd studied to perfect her Fjerdan and her knowledge of their culture. It had been a way of preparing herself for them, for the battle to come. And Jarl Brum was the worst of them. He was a legend, the monster waiting in the dark." (Chapter 14, Page 168)

While the Fjerdan drüskelle, *or Grisha hunters,*
perceive the Grisha as monsters, Grisha like Nina take
the opposite view. Even as the Fjerdans see themselves
as wiping out demonic Grisha, for Grisha the drüskelle
are the monstrous "creatures of [...] nightmares."
Humans define one another as monsters based on a
lack of empathy and understanding, and not because
some groups or individuals are actually less human
than others. The characterization of drüskelle *leader*
Jarl Brum as the "worst" of the monsters is
particularly significant, as readers come to learn that
Brum is a mentor to Matthias, Nina's enemy turned
lover.

9. "Matthias had always fought his own decency. To
    become a *drüskelle,* he'd had to kill the good things
    inside him. But the boy he should have been was
    always there, and she'd begun to see the truth of him in
    the days they'd spent together after the shipwreck. She
    wanted to believe that boy was still there, locked away,
    despite her betrayal and whatever he'd endured at
    Hellgate." (Chapter 14, Page 174)

    In this quote, Bardugo wrestles with the question of
    how humans become monstrous, and she suggests that
    experiences of violence and suffering can cause humans
    to "kill the good things inside" them. Without "good
    things" such as compassion and a basic respect for
    others, humans can act like monsters. However,
    monstrosity is a mask rather than a true self, and here
    Nina hopes that the "decency" of Matthias's true
    character has managed to survive beneath the mask.

10. "'A monster, a maiden, a sylph of the ice. You kissed me, whispered stories in my ear. You sang to me and held me as I slept. Your laugh chased me into waking.'
'You always hated my laugh.'
'I loved your laugh, Nina. And your fierce warrior's heart. I might have loved you, too.'
Might have. Once. Before she had betrayed him. Those words carved an ache into her chest." (Chapter 14, 175)

For Matthias, Nina is both a monster, a Grisha with unnatural powers, and a temptress, a "sylph of the ice." Matthias must choose between the doctrines he's received from the drüskelle, *who treated him like family yet told him the Grisha were evil, and his love for Nina. Nina feels deeply for Matthias—she aches to realize she's betrayed him, even if unintentionally, as her testimony landed him in prison, and she was unable to free him. When the characters listen to their emotions rather than exterior messages, they see each other's humanity instead of a monstrous mask.*

11. "Feeling anything for Kaz Brekker was the worst kind of foolishness. She knew that. But he'd been the one to rescue her, to see her potential. He'd bet on her, and that meant something—even if he'd done it for his own selfish reasons. He'd even dubbed her the Wraith. [...] He'd helped her build a legend to wear as armor, something bigger and more frightening than the girl she'd been." (Chapter 16, Pages 188-89)

Characters must construct new identities to survive in a cruel world, and these identities often prevent deeper connection. After being kidnapped and sold to a

*brothel, Inej needs to wear "armor," to become
frightening so she won't remain vulnerable. Kaz has
donned his own armor: the appearance that he acts
purely for selfish reasons, that he will act cruelly to
protect himself. In a world where teenagers must
completely hide their vulnerabilities, caring for
someone the way Inej does for Kaz becomes
foolishness, a pointless endeavor that can only lead to
disappointment.*

12. "'What do you want, then?'
The old answers came easily to mind. Money.
Vengeance. Jordie's voice in my head silenced forever.
But a different reply roared to life inside him, loud,
insistent, and unwelcome. You, Inej. You." (Chapter
18, Page 205)

*Kaz's life goal has become avenging his brother's
death; however, Kaz finds that no matter how he tries
to deny his unwelcome, vulnerable human side, his love
for Inej only makes it more powerful. Bardugo suggests
that love for others will ultimately win out over the
violent desire for vengeance.*

13. "What had he said to Geels at the Exchange? *I'm the
kind of bastard they only manufacture in the Barrel.*
One more lie, one more piece of the myth he'd built for
himself." (Chapter 18, Page 205)

*Kaz's constructed identity—he's presented himself as a
cruel, even monstrous creature born from a violent
environment—adds to the novel's theme of home and
family. While many other characters in the novel long
to return to their homes, Kaz actively resists his home*

to the point of erasing its very existence. At the same time, the family Kaz has tragically lost actually shapes his new identity: Kaz remakes himself as a "bastard" of the criminal underworld to achieve revenge for his brother's death.

14. "The first day trekking was like a cleansing—little talk, the white hush of the north welcoming Matthias back without judgment. He'd expected more complaints, but even Wylan had simply put his head down and walked. *They're all survivors*, Matthias understood. *They adapt.*" (Chapter 19, Page 219)

    In the novel's world, teenagers must adapt to losing their homelands and families in various ways. Matthias feels welcomed back to his own home of Fjerda, which he was forced out of following a shipwreck after already losing his family to a Grisha attack. Just as Matthias had to adapt to life in Hellgate prison, the other members of the Dregs must now adapt to a bitterly cold, foreign landscape. These teens are all survivors who rely on their own strength; this fact draws them together, allowing them to find a new sense of family.

15. "'Because our crime is *existing*. Our crime is what we are.'
    Matthias went quiet, and when he spoke he was caught between shame for what he was about to say and the need to speak the words, the words he'd been raised on, the words that still rang true for him. 'Nina, has it ever occurred to you that maybe … you weren't meant to exist?'" (Chapter 19, Page 232)

*Indoctrinated prejudice can lead humans to view each
other as monsters, as beings without the right to exist.
Matthias's shame reveals his inner knowledge that his
belief may not be accurate—after all, he loves Nina,
one of the Grisha he's been told aren't meant to exist,
but his inherited beliefs are clearly strong and
dangerous ones. Only by looking past labels like
"witch" and "monster," and seeing others as
individuals, can characters like Matthias move beyond
prejudice to form deeper connections.*

16. "'Zoya Nazyalensky?'
Nina had stopped short. 'You know her?
'We all know of her. She's a powerful witch.'
It had hit her then: For the drüskelle, Zoya was a little
like Jarl Brum—cruel, inhuman, the thing that waited in
the dark with death in her hands. Zoya was this boy's
monster. The thought left her uneasy." (Chapter 20,
Page 236)

*Nina realizes that the woman she looked up to as
mentor and family is a "monster" to the* drüskelle, *just
as Brum, Matthias's mentor, is Nina's "monster";
monsters are created by the perspective of those who
perceive and label them. This realization makes Nina
uneasy because, if Zoya is not a monster, then Brum
one can't be either. Her enemies, like her mentors, are
simply humans who choose to act in ways that help or
harm others.*

17. "'This must be hard for you,' [Inej] said quietly. 'To be
here but not really be home.'
[Matthias] looked down at his cup. 'You have no idea.'
'I think I do. I haven't seen my home in a long time.'

Kaz turned away and began chatting with Jesper. He seemed to do that whenever she mentioned going back to Ravka. Of course, Inej couldn't be certain she'd find her parents there. Suli were travelers. For them, 'home' really just meant family." (Chapter 21, Pages 264-65)

All the novel's main characters have experienced the loss of home, either a place, the people they cared for, or both. This loss actually provides them with a new connection, as here, Matthias and Inej find common ground over the fact they've been separated from home for so long. Even now that Matthias has returned to his homeland, he's not really home, not with the people he once cared about, and the author suggests that characters can't truly return to the communities they've lost. They've been transformed by violence and suffering, and they must find a new community with those who share and understand their experiences.

18. "He had survived the fever, but he might well die out here on the Reaper's Barge. Did he care? There was nothing waiting for him in the city but more hunger and dark alleys and the damp of the canals. Even as he thought it, he knew it wasn't true. Vengeance was waiting, vengeance for Jordie and maybe for himself, too." (Chapter 22, Pages 275-76)

This quotation marks the moment Kaz first conceives of the desire for vengeance that drives him to become Dirtyhands and propels his decisions for much of the novel. Kaz wants to make the criminals of the Barrel suffer—most of all, gang leader Pekka—for taking everything from Kaz and leaving him at the point where

*he has nothing but "hunger and dark alleys" and pain
ahead of him. Righteous anger gives Kaz something to
live for and forces him to transform, but he must
become one with the "dark alleys and the damp of the
canals," the worst aspects of the city that has destroyed
him.*

19. "She wanted a storm—thunder, wind, a deluge. She
wanted it to crash through Ketterdam's pleasure houses,
lifting roofs and tearing doors off their hinges. She
wanted it to raise the seas, take hold of every slaving
ship, shatter their masts, and smash their hulls against
unforgiving shores. *I want to call that storm,* she
thought. [...] She would hunt the slavers and their
buyers. They would learn to fear her, and they would
know her by her name." (Chapter 25, Page 311)

*In contrast to Kaz's dark, violent quest for revenge, Inej
conceives of a vengeance that will save both others and
her. Like Kaz, Inej rejects her status as a victim and
looks for a way to become as powerful as the ones who
victimized her, but she does so without taking on the
victimizers' cruelty as Kaz has done. Inej conceives of a
more powerful version of herself, one who commands
"a deluge," and she will use her power to save others
from being victimized.*

20. "The swim back from the Reaper's Barge had been
Kaz's rebirth. The child he'd been had died of firepox.
The fever had burned away every gentle thing inside
him.
Survival wasn't nearly as hard as he'd thought once he
left decency behind. The first rule was to find someone

smaller and weaker and take what he had." (Chapter 26, Page 313)

A cruel world, and in particular one that doesn't protect children, causes its people to lose their humanity. After undergoing suffering, loss, and betrayal, and being tossed in a pile of corpses with no one caring enough to notice he was still alive, Kaz had every gentle aspect of himself destroyed. To survive, he became like the people who victimized him, as he set aside his decency to take advantage of the small and weak. Kaz has made himself into a monster, and while he's managed to survive, he's lost his human compassion as a result.

21. "What bound them together? Greed? Desperation? Was it just the knowledge that if one or all of them disappeared tonight, no one would come looking? Inej's mother and father might still shed tears for the daughter they'd lost, but if Inej died tonight, there would be no one to grieve for the girl she was now. She had no family, no parents or siblings, only people to fight beside. Maybe that was something to be grateful for, too." (Chapter 28, Page 332)

Through misfortune or the cruelty of others, every main character has been separated from their family and home, but they've found each other. No one outside of these six characters' world can understand the tougher versions of themselves they've been forced to become; they truly have only each other, and for Inej, that's "something to be grateful for."

22. "More than any place in the Ice Court, more than any place in the world, this felt like home to him. But it was home turned on its head, his life viewed at the wrong angle." (Chapter 29, Page 343)

As Matthias discovers, none of these characters can truly go home again. Every character has dealt with suffering, transformed, and learned to see the world in a new way; as a result, home doesn't look the same or hold the same meaning. Matthias's relationship with Nina has shown him the error of his former family's viewpoint. Matthias, and the other characters, will have to choose whether to continue to approach their old homes from the wrong angle or to find new homes with the people who understand their struggles.

23. "[Matthias] thought of Nina standing terrified in that cell as the door slammed shut. He had longed to see her made captive, punished as he had been punished. And yet, after everything they'd been through, he was not surprised by the pain he felt at seeing it come to pass." (Chapter 35, Page 381)

The desire for revenge crumbles beneath the strength of compassion and love. Now that Matthias sees Nina as a human rather than a witch—and more than that, a human he admires and loves—he can't take pleasure in her suffering. Matthias's love for Nina, and his choice to rescue her rather than seeking vengeance, will bring him much greater satisfaction.

24. "[Kaz] tried to think of his brother, of revenge, of Pekka Rollins tied to a chair in the house on Zelverstraat, trade orders stuffed down his throat as Kaz

forced him to remember Jordie's name. But all he could think of was Inej [...] He needed to tell her ... what? That she was lovely and brave and better than anything he deserved. That he was twisted, crooked, wrong, but not so broken that he couldn't pull himself together into some semblance of a man for her." (Chapter 38, page 403)

Like Matthias, Kaz finds love more powerful than revenge. While revenge is a negative impulse that brings out violence and cruelty, love for Inej makes Kaz want to become a better version of himself, a man rather than a broken monster.

25. "Inej had wanted Kaz to become someone else, a better person, a gentler thief. But that boy had no place here. That boy ended up starving in an alley. He ended up dead. That boy couldn't get her back.

    I'm going to get my money, Kaz vowed. *And I'm going to get my girl.* Inej could never be his, not really, but he would find a way to give her the freedom he'd promised her so long ago.
    Dirtyhands had come to see the rough work done."
    (Chapter 45, Page 456)

    Kaz finds that as much as he wanted to become a better person for Inej, the cruel world of the Barrel will force him to again embrace his darker nature. Kaz has been duped again, and once again his enemy has taken the person Kaz loves most. The novel ends where it began, with revenge propelling Kaz forward, turning him into the monster Dirtyhands.

1. *Six of Crows* is told from the points of view of five out of six different characters who join together to complete a mission. How do the characters' voices differ, and how are they similar? How does the polyphony of voices affect the reader's experience? Why do you think the author chooses not to narrate a chapter from Wylan's point of view?

2. Two principal characters in *Six of Crows*, Kaz and Inej, also go by the respective nicknames Dirtyhands and the Wraith. How do these characters' nicknamed personas differ from their true selves? How do their dual identities transform over time and reflect larger themes in the novel?

3. The Dregs' motto is "No mourners, no funerals." How do you think this phrase came about, and what does it say about the Dregs' world? How does the meaning behind the motto change throughout the novel?

4. Each main character has a different motivation for joining the team's prison-break mission. Choose one character and examine their motivation in depth. How do their desires reflect larger themes of the novel? How do their priorities change as the events of the book unfold?

5. Throughout *Six of Crows*, characters mourn the loss of their homelands and search for a way to return. How do the characters' definitions of "home" change throughout the novel? Does each character ultimately

find a home, or are they still searching at the end of the novel?

6. Examine the theme and symbolism of monsters throughout the novel. Which characters are portrayed as monsters, and how does the definition of monsters change according to different characters' points of view?

7. What role does *jurda parem* play in the novel? Does *parem*'s influence have any similarities to the effects of drugs in our world? In what ways does *parem* differ from real-life drugs? Why do you think the author chose to describe the drug as she did?

8. *Six of Crows* includes characters of different ethnicities, as well as characters who are persecuted for their magical abilities. How do the novels' categorizations relate to the treatment of different ethnic and cultural groups in the real world? What real-world situations parallel the Grisha's plight?

9. The main characters in *Six of Crows* often make immoral choices, and none could be characterized as traditional heroes. Why do you think Bardugo chose a crew of antiheroes to populate her novels? How do her characters redeem themselves by the novel's end?

10. The novel ends with Kaz's crew having completed their mission but finding themselves double-crossed by the merchant who hired them. How does this ending reflect the world Bardugo has created? Do you think the

protagonists' mission was still worthwhile, and did they accomplish what they set out to do?

Made in the USA
Monee, IL
28 May 2021